# Grandma Series III

## GRANDMA'S FAVORITE STORIES

LYDIA BONGCARON WADE

authorHOUSE®

*AuthorHouse™*
*1663 Liberty Drive*
*Bloomington, IN 47403*
*www.authorhouse.com*
*Phone: 1 (800) 839-8640*

*Published by AuthorHouse 07/29/2016*

*ISBN: 978-1-5246-1839-1 (sc)*
*ISBN: 978-1-5246-1838-4 (e)*

*Print information available on the last page.*

*Any people depicted in stock imagery provided by Thinkstock are models, and such images are being used for illustrative purposes only. Certain stock imagery © Thinkstock.*

*This book is printed on acid-free paper.*

Grandma Lydia with Olivia and Brian

# GRANDMA SERIES III

### "Grandma's Favorite Stories

### (A Memoir)

Grandchildren are the sweetest, priceless, dearest beings;

And grandparents simply adore them.

To my Grandchildren: Stephanie, Alexandra, Gabriella, Olivia and Brian

"When I was Small!"

My father's hands, my mother's embrace, they were my guide, my

comfort, when I was small.

Dark nights became bright, the days were pure delight, full of love!

When I was small.

People were all merry, all friendly, what we had we shared abundantly.

When I was small.

Fiesta days, the best of all! Celebrations abound, joyful days,

glorious nights;

Music blaring, feet untiring gracefully dancing, children playing,

loudly laughing, happiness unending !

When I was small !

By Grandma Lydia

# PART I

# Grandma's Fantasy Tales

## CHAPTER 1

As the "Empire Builder" train originating from Union Station, Chicago slid slowly into the Orlando, Florida Station on a sunny Saturday afternoon in April, Grandma Lydia peered anxiously outside the window of her train car. She did not see Angela, her daughter in-law and her two grandchildren, Olivia and Brian on the platform. She picked up her hand luggage and exited the train along with the other passengers. She collected her checked in luggage from the conductor hurriedly. The train was pulling out of the station in ten minutes.

She scanned the faces of the people around the platform who were happy meeting their friends or loved ones, or waving goodbye to the departing passengers. There was no sign of the three she was expecting to meet her. Grandma went inside the waiting lounge and settled down on a bench. Angela and the children were perhaps held by traffic on their way to the station, she thought. Just as she was about to call Angela's cell phone number, she felt a tug on her sleeve.

"Hi! Grandma!" A familiar girl's voice greeted her. She came face to face with her granddaughter, Olivia. Her brother Brian stood behind her, pouting. She hugged them lovingly. Brian refused to be hugged at first. He was always very shy. During her last visit several months ago, he ran away from her.

"Where's your mother?" "Welcome, Mom!"

It was Angela who answered her query. She kissed

grandma's cheek. Grandma returned her kiss." I was

going to call you at the public phone, but the line is

long." She pointed to the telephone booth at the other

side of the waiting lounge. I forgot to charge my cell

phone. We did not see you getting off the train. How

was your train trip?"

"Not bad, not bad at all. In fact, I enjoyed it.

That was a long trip from Chicago Union Station to

here. We had a change of trains in Washington D.C. I

spent two and a half days on the train, but it was fun

and a new kind of experience for me. The train was

very comfortable and I felt safe. Next time, I am going to travel by rail again. It takes longer but it is relaxing and with lesser hassle. I am tired of flying too."

Angela followed grandma to the kitchen after dinner that night and said," Mom, I shall be leaving the house at 4:30 in the afternoon tomorrow. I would like you to go to Pollo Tropicale for dinner with the children and their baby sitter, Jasmine before I leave. I do not want them to see me go and cry, especially Brian."

"How many days does Jasmine come during the week?" She comes daily, goes home after taking the kids to school, comes back at 3:30 p.m. and stays overnight when I am on night duty. She is off during weekends when I am home. Her schedule is on the bulletin board." Grandma followed her to the bulletin board on one side of the kitchen.

"Mom, the children love to play in the park during Saturday afternoons. Make sure you bring along bottled water. The water fountain in the park is out of order. And mom, please do not give them candies and sodas. The refrigerator and the shelves in the pantry are full of healthy snacks. She had listed do's, don'ts and reminders, which she posted side by side with Jasmine's schedule.

Angela was very thorough and concerned. This was the first time she would leave the children at home. She did not want to leave her precious children entirely in the care of the babysitter for one whole week, a good babysitter though she was. Grandma was the only person she could entrust them to completely. Grandma refused to accept the money Angela gave her for the children's expenses. "Leave everything to me, dear. I would be happy to take care of everything while you are away. Your Medical Conference in L.A. would only be for one week. You would be back here next Sunday at 7:00 p.m., according to the itinerary you sent me."

"Bye, mom. Enjoy with the kids." Angela kissed her mother in-law, Olivia then Brian before they all piled into the SUV with Jasmine at the wheel the following afternoon. Angela headed upstairs and took out her luggage from the locked closet. She had made sure the children did not see her pack her things for the trip. She was hesitant to attend the Doctors' Conference in Los Angeles at first. On the other hand, she was also eager to learn new trends in her chosen field. When she passed the Board Examinations in Internal Medicine a year ago, she applied for and got accepted for a gynecologist position at St. Francis Hospital in Orlando. She would take up the position before the end of the year. The salary and benefits were better than what she was getting presently as a General Practitioner.

Angela and grandma's son Clyde were divorced two years ago. His job abroad as Computer Architect required too much traveling and long separation. It had taken a toll on their relationship. It was a difficult time for both of them but they had run out of alternatives. They also had opposite views on job and family matters. The efforts to compromise did not work. Eventually, Clyde moved his family from Naperville, Illinois to Orlando, Florida before the divorce was finalized. He later on moved to Detroit.

Grandma agonized seeing the break up, but there was nothing she could do to prevent the divorce. Grown-up, married children in this country have complete control of whatever direction their family relationship took. Grandma wished her son and his family was living in her original country wherein divorce was not allowed. In her time, families endeavored, endured and resolved their differences and stayed together. She sympathized with Angela especially that she was alone in America. Her family lived in Romania. So when Angela asked her to babysit for Olivia and Brian for one week, she readily accepted, leaving her two dogs with a dog sitter.

Angela and her children, Olivia and Brian

# CHAPTER 2

Olivia and Brian cried when they learned that their mom had gone for a trip related to her job. Grandma had a hard time calming them down, especially Brian who took a longer time to stop. She took them out again that evening to the movies. "The Sound of Music" soothed them but when they got home, Brian cried again. Jasmine went home to get her two children who were almost as old as the two kids to play with Olivia and Brian. They all spent the night at Angela's home.

"Tomorrow, we shall go to the Children's Museum, then spend the rest of the afternoon in the park. You can eat all the ice cream you want too at Ben and Jerry's." Grandma was putting the children to bed on the second night of Angela's absence. This was part of her appeasement tactics. She saw Brian rubbing his eyes. She knew he was about to cry again. She immediately went to his side of the king size bed and put her arm around him.

"No, no. I don't like museums. I like to go to the farm to see the ponies and ride on one of them."

"But sweetheart, the farm is very far from here, more than 30 miles. I doubt if Jasmine will drive us that far. What about if we see a cowboy movie, ha? You like the toy miniature horses that your auntie Bing gave you, don't you? Let's see them in the movie, running with handsome cowboys riding them." She stroked the boy's hair and kissed him.

"Grandma, grandma," Olivia was urgently tugging at her grandma's night gown sleeves. I would like us to go to Toys R Us. My best friend in school showed me a new Barbie Doll. It was very pretty. I want something new to add to my collection. The two children bickered for a while. "My darlings, calm down. We shall go to both places after church tomorrow. Shall we sleep now? It is past 9 o'clock. Mommy said we should go to bed at 8:30. Let's say our "Angel of God" prayer first." Brian cried again when he remembered mommy."Hush, hush, my brave boy. Mommy will call again tomorrow for sure." Grandma held Brian and rocked him to sleep. Olivia had long gone to sleep before Brian slept at last. Grandma slept in the middle of the two children in their king size bed.

Angela called every night after supper time. Olivia and Brian would insist to speak with their mommy first. Brian always had the upper hand. Poor

Olivia could not stand her brother's screaming if she spoke to their mother before him. Sometimes the two would hold the receiver together, listen and spoke to their mommy at the same time. Often, grandma did not have the chance to speak to Angela.

"What would you like to do tonight, my dear ones? They were having noodles and fried chicken for dinner, which grandma cooked herself. Brian liked the fine, rice noodles more than the other recipes that grandma prepared. Olivia put down the leg of chicken on her plate and said," Please read "Cinderella" to me, grandma. I love that story."

"I like to see the DVD's that uncle Ariel gave me. Brian ran to the Family room and came back to the dining table with three DVD's. Two were dog stories. One was a farmer's boy story. He chose the dog story first, entitled, "My Dog Skippy." I would like to see the farmer's boy story too, after this one." You can watch only one DVD tonight, Brian. This dog story is two hours long. You will watch the other one tomorrow night. We have to go to bed early. Tomorrow is a school day."

While Brian was watching his movie, Olivia took out the Cinderella book from the shelf. She settled down on the couch with grandma when all the dishes had been put away. "Why do you like this Cinderella story, sweetie?" "Oh, I like stories about girls, princesses, kingdoms and fairies." Grandma pondered for one moment. Now she knew what the little girl liked. "What about if I told you stories which my mother used to tell me and my sisters during bedtimes when we were children? They were mostly about enchanted creatures, palaces, kings, queens, princes and princesses."

"Oh, yes, grandma, I should like to hear them. Mommy seldom ever tells us bedtime stories because she is always tired from work. Sometimes she falls asleep before we do." "All right then. We shall start the storytelling tomorrow. Do you think your brother would like storytelling?" "Sometimes he does, but he gets bored easily. He sleeps before the story ends, that's why mommy does not tell stories often. But I like storytelling."

"Why don't you start tonight, grandma? I would like to hear the stories that your mother used to tell. What was her name? "Just call her your great grandma. I shall tell you about your great grandparents before we start our storytelling tomorrow." Grandma read the Cinderella story to her granddaughter. Olivia stayed awake until the end of the story.

# CHAPTER 3

## The Lost Prince

The children had an early dinner. They settled down beside grandma on the couch. Brian was watching his DVD, but joined them on the couch when grandma told him that she had a

very interesting story to tell. Brian also wanted to

share the bowl of hot popcorn his sister was holding.

Grandma had promised earlier to give him a nice

prize if he listened to her stories with her sister.

"Long, long time ago, when there were no

movies, telephones, cell phones, books, toys and

other things which children enjoy today, there was a

large kingdom ruled by an old, kind king. His name was King Gerard and his beautiful, young wife was Queen Stefa. She was once a very pretty princess, the only daughter of a French monarch. Their kingdom was situated along a long stretch of white beaches. The castle, which was painted in bright red was built on top of a hill overlooking the blue ocean. High cliffs bounded the castle on its three sides facing the ocean. The cliffs were so high that a strong boulder thrown from the summit would break into pieces before hitting the bottom. The medieval castle could be reached from the outside world only through a wide road enclosed with strong, steel fences bordered with high, pointed tops.

From the sea, the castle looked enchanting as it was formidable and mysterious. In the early morning mist, it appeared like a fair maiden rising from the sea, revealing her full splendor and breathtaking beauty when seen in the middle of the day, then fades slowly in the creeping twilight. At night, instead of disappearing into the gloom, the castle glittered with a thousand torches, lighting every corner of its six inches thick stone walls and massive pillars. It was a magical castle in every sense inside and outside.

Approaching through the single intimidating entrance, one had to stop well behind the draw bridge over a roaring, fast-moving creek 20 ft. below. Thick, steel bars with tips like arrows lifted as the door opened if the guest or guests were expected or properly identified. It stayed firmly closed otherwise. A high-pitched bell would toll if one stepped into the bridge connecting the castle to the wide landing if not cleared for entrance. Heavily armed guards in armor and helmets stood outside and inside the doors.

The king had no known enemies but several times in the past, the castle was the object of invasions by pirates and foreign marauders. The kingdom was known to be full of riches. Money, gold, silver, and other precious gems attracted local fortune hunters and lured thieves from across the seas and distant lands. Only one attempt so far came closer to the formidable fortress, which was easily repelled by the king's soldiers. King Gerard had an army of over a thousand battle-hardened soldiers, spies and scouts. He also had faithful allies spread across the countryside. The kingdom was as secure and as safe as most of the castles and kingdoms during that period, perhaps even more.

It took the king and his queen long to have a child. They almost gave up hope that they would ever have one. So when their first born, a boy was born, there was a huge celebration in the castle attended by kings, princes, princesses and other royals from near and far. The festivities lasted for one week, characterized by jousts, tournaments, games and plays, magic, dancing and music.

Prince Leonard grew up to be the most handsome boy parents could have as a son. His parents doted on him, their most precious gem, far more precious than all their jewels combined. Pampered lavishly by his loving parents and tutored by a very obliging and conniving governess, the prince turned out most naughty, obnoxious

and cruel. At six years old, he struck a soldier with his

own sword when he failed to bow to him, then spat

on the soldier's dead body. He chased a maidservant

around the palace grounds and shoved her face into

the pool, drowning her. Her only fault was being ugly.

At ten years old, he had his horse trainer trampled

by his new pony when the poor man was not quick enough to hand him the pony's reins. He resorted to continuous tantrums, driving everyone crazy when he did not get what he wanted. Everybody hated and feared him, except his parents.

Prince Leonard was a demon of a boy. He did what he wanted to do, said what he wanted to say and took what he desired without so much as a look of disapproval from anybody around him. His parents tolerated him, always looked the other way and ignored the complaints of his subjects. Once during dinner, the boy threw an empty glass at his father, the king, when the latter forbade him to drink a glass of strong wine. When his mother rebuked him, he went around to her at the other side of the table and emptied a glass of red wine into her white robe. Instead of getting upset, the royal parents only laughed. Nothing could make them mad at their precocious, precious son. After all, they could not have another child. Their fortune teller had told them the sad news with finality.

One day at the age of eighteen, when Prince Leonard went with palace guests on a hunting trip, he got separated from the group. His two bodyguards went to look for him but when they found him, the prince dismissed them. He wanted to be on his own. He was tired of being watched all the time. The soldiers were scared to say no to him so they left him

alone to himself and they rejoined the hunting group.

Alone for the first time, Prince Leonard rode

aimlessly, enjoying his new found independence.

When he got weary, he rested on the bank of a shallow

river. Its clear, inviting water quenched his thirst. The

soft murmuring of the water as it flowed towards the

lush meadows downstream lulled him to sleep. The

sun had gone down when he opened his eyes again.

Soon, the thick forests around him became ominous

shadows. He decided to leave and head back to the

palace. He was now feeling the first pangs of hunger.

But which way was it back ? He did not keep track

of where he had started. Darkness descended around him fast. He could not see anything farther than a yard. The howling of wild animals in the forest terrified him. He began to panic.

A sound behind him jolted his confused mind. He raised his sword in readiness without knowing what kind of danger he was facing. The trampling sound came from his left, becoming louder and louder as it came closer. Suddenly, a heavy, hairy body of a huge animal jumped on him, clawing at his chest. A leopard! He tried to raise his sword but his whole body was pinned down. His sword fell off his hand as he struggled to fight the animal. In the darkness, he could see the creature's bright eyes focused on him, while it started to nibble at his arm. His loud cries were lost in the wide expanse of the deserted forest. The leopard was aiming at his neck now. He was losing his consciousness when the light of torches illumined the bushes around the hapless prince. He faintly heard the leopard groan as it released its unfortunate victim.

Prince Leonard awoke inside a small hut, surrounded by a group of curious people. The prince squinted at the bright rays of the morning sun penetrating through a window. He could not see very well although the sun's rays shone directly above his wooden bed. He could not move his body. It hurt all over badly. He slept again without disturbance. In the middle of the night, he was screaming. He had a nightmare. The huge leopard was tearing up his whole body until nothing was left of him except his royal clothes.

"Please calm down. It was only a bad dream." A young girl of about sixteen was holding his hand. Two elderly persons stood behind her. "Here, have something to eat." The elderly woman approached his bed holding a small bowl of some hot soup. The elderly man came around and examined his wounds. It hurt but Prince Leonard was so hungry to mind the pain the man's hand caused as he opened his bandages.

"Where am I?" "You are in Yoona village. We are friends. You are safe now."The girl spoke again. We killed the leopard who attacked you. You may see his skin hanging up there at a shed outside." The girl smiled as she gave him a glass of water. "Who are you?" The prince asked in a low voice. "I am Ela and these are my parents, Joso and Ena." The prince struggled to get up but the man restrained him. "And what may be your name, lad?' The elderly man asked. Obviously they did not recognize him. He thought for one moment.

"I am Sauro, a hunter from a far village. Where are my clothes? He decided to withhold his identity.

Who knows they might be enemies or unscrupulous peasants who could be after his kingdom's wealth?" "They were in shreds. We left them in the forest." The girl answered, adjusting the old but clean sheets covering his body. "I am very grateful. You saved my life. My whole body would have fully satisfied the hungry beast." "It could have caused him indigestion too." The girl had a sense of humor. Her parents laughed heartily. Prince Leonard joined the laughter weakly. The kindhearted family left him as he closed his eyes again.

Prince Leonard had a dream that night. An old fairy appeared to him and said, "I sent the leopard to teach you a lesson. You are a bad prince. Unless you reform, you will never get back to your kingdom. You will serve this family whom I sent to save you from the leopard. They are kind, humble people. You will learn their ways in the village and remain until it's time for you to go back to your kingdom." Prince Leonard did not know what it all meant.

The prince recovered from his wounds fast. The herbal medications they gave him helped a lot. An old, wise quack woman came to him every day and ministered to his wounds. The girl seldom left his side. She brought his food regularly and helped him as he hopped around his hut. When he was strong enough, she brought him outside in the sunshine. He realized

he was in a tiny village with nice, friendly people

who were quick to offer help in whatever way they

could. They were happy people although they were

very poor. They were mostly farmers and hunters.

Occasionally, when hunting trips were very

successful, there were celebrations with music from

native instruments and dancing throughout the night.

There were tournaments and jousts using crude swords

and lances. Even women participated in the wrestling

competitions. The prince was quite happy in this

simple, primitive life. He learned to chop wood, catch

fish and wild chickens, cultivate the soil, plant corn

and other crops. Ela taught him to cook simple meals and roast his catch over live coals.

Prince Leonard lived among his rescuers for a couple of years and became an entirely different person. His arrogance and cruelty turned into kindness. Each time he wanted to get angry, something prodded him to be considerate and patient. It was a force so strong and compelling. The fairy's words would ring in his ears and remind him that he was on probation.

He longed to go back to his kingdom. How? He learned that there was a castle across the sea many miles away from the village. They said it was ruled by an old king who just died. The queen was very sickly and was rumored to follow the king soon if not cured. She suffered from a strange malady nobody knew how to cure. They also mentioned about a prince who disappeared in a hunting trip and was believed eaten by ferocious beasts. Prince Leonard became more anxious to leave the village, the place he had learned to love.

One night after many more months, the fairy appeared to him again in his dream. "You may now go back to your palace. Your mother needs you and the kingdom needs a King. Tomorrow morning before the sun rises, go down to the edge of the river. You will find a boat moored at its bank. Take Ela and her parents with you. The boat will take you all the way to the sea then to the beach near your palace. There, you will be met by a horse-drawn carriage accompanied by six soldiers. The carriage will take you to the palace. You will rule your kingdom with justice, kindness and generosity to your subjects with Ela, your queen."

Prince Leonard did as he was told by the fairy. He took Ela, her mother and father with him and they rode on the boat for three days. When they finally reached the castle, there was a big welcome waiting for them. Leonard's mother became well again from her mysterious illness. A grand wedding took place and the celebrations lasted for one month.

A prince and a princess were born to King Leonard and Queen Ela and they lived happily ever after. That's the end of my story tonight. Did you two like it? "Grandma, I would like to be a prince one day." Brian was surprisingly fully awake throughout the story telling. "Sweetheart, there are no more princes, kings and queens now, or kingdoms. But I will buy you a prince' outfit at the Medieval Store. It will be your prize, Brian for being such a good boy"."Grandma, I love your story! Can you tell us another story tomorrow, grandma? Olivia was yawning. "I will. Now let's go to bed."

# CHAPTER 4

## The Sad Boy

Brian sat on grandma's lap as his sister went to get the bowl of popcorn from Jasmine. The latter was preparing to go home on the third afternoon of grandma's arrival. "What is your story tonight, grandma?" Olivia asked settling down close to grandma and Brian. "I think you two will like my story tonight, darlings. Brian, the popcorn is still very hot. Wait a second." Grandma took a s smaller bowl from the kitchen, put some in the bowl and gave it to

Brian. Olivia settled on the other side of her grandma

with the bigger bowl of popcorn.

"A family of five, the mother, father and three

children lived in a valley with several other families.

Susie, 10, Jean, 8 and Jonny,6 years old would go out

into the nearby meadow to pick berries and apples

for their mother who made jellies and jams out of

them almost every afternoon after school. The valley

was lush with green grass, flowering shrubs, and

shady trees. Nearly every house had fruit trees and

flowering plants in their front and in their backyards.

The McBride family had their own fruit trees and

flowering plants and shrubs too, but the children

would go out beyond their own home and into the

outlying woods to search for mushrooms and berries

and to pick some wild flowers too. They also loved to

chase butterflies.

"Do not go deep into the woods, children.

You might get lost. Remember Greta, our neighbor's

daughter who was lost and never came back home?"

Their mother, Jenna cautioned them. The children

would always listen to their mother. The family was

closely knit. Their father Dan worked in the city as

clerk in the City Hall and Jenna was a midwife, but

her husband preferred her to be a full time mother and

housewife. The McBride family was a typical, middle class family known in their village as a model family. Jenna would sometimes volunteer in the village clinic when they needed an extra hand. During his off hours, Dan would also volunteer to teach the young boys in the village, Music during weekends. Dan inherited his love of music from his father. He could play several wind instruments and the piano as well.

The two children, Jean and Jonny were picking mushrooms when they saw big butterflies hovering around the blueberry bushes. They were very pretty with multi-colored wings, silver, red, blue and green. The children were fascinated and decided to try to catch them. They put down their baskets half full of

mushrooms and went after the colorful creatures.

"Jean, Jonny! Mother is calling for supper!"

They heard their older sister Susie, but the younger

children continued with their preoccupation. Jean

caught the one she was pursuing. "Jonny, I just

caught one big butterfly. I think it is the biggest

one. Let's go home now. Jonny? Jean looked around

her but she could not see her brother. She called

again, and then again, each time louder and louder.

But the boy was nowhere around her. Jean became

frantic. She searched the bushes, crawling through

the shrubs and the vines, unmindful of the thorns.

No sign of the boy. He just vanished into thin air.

Jean sobbed.

Just then, Susie came, looking annoyed. "I had

been calling you two. Are you deaf? Supper is waiting

and mother said to hurry. Why are you crying? Where's

your brother?" Jean started to cry loudly. "I could not

find Jonny. He just disappeared." She wailed. "What?

Where would he be?" Susie and Jean searched and searched until it was almost twilight. They left, scared to remain in the woods in the dark.

"Let's go home and tell our parents. They would know what to do."" When they got home,. they told their mother what happened. Their father was in the dog pen feeding their Labrador. When he learned of Jonny's disappearance, he left the house without eating and went to the village manager to ask for help. Soon, a group of half a dozen villagers set out into the woods and began the search, with torches and flashlights. They scoured the outlying woodland taking along three dogs to pick up Jonny's scent. They spread out to cover a wider area and searched until

after midnight.

"Let us call off the search for now and resume

tomorrow. It will be easier to navigate this forest in the

bright sunlight," the manager declared. Jonny's family

was sleepless throughout the night. "How would

Jonny survive in the cold autumn night? What if he

was devoured by some wild animals that sometimes

roam closer to the village? They all had the same

morbid thoughts.

The search was resumed the following day and

continued for a week, but their efforts were fruitless.

There was no clue as to what really happened to

the boy. The village folk decided to burn down the wooded areas around the village for up to a mile radius. Strict village ordinance was enforced. Children were no longer allowed to venture even into the clearings. There was a general feeling of dread and apprehension among the parents and elders. This was a third disappearance of a child after all. The first was a teenage boy who wandered into the woods alone but never came back. The second was a girl of four, who was with the mother at the time but disappeared suddenly when the mother turned her back from her when she was picking strawberries.

A group of beautiful fairies gathered around a boy of 6. They were fussing around him, teasing him and making him laugh. They offered him many toys, all strange and new. They served him an array of tempting, delicious foods. They put him on a big, thick cushioned bed and sang beautiful hymns to him, accompanied with a lyre. "I want to go home! I need my mom, my sisters and my dad!" He continued to wail. The fairies had a meeting. They wondered why this boy would want to go home. The other children who joined them were quite happy. This one was sad and restless. They decided to return the boy to his family. There was no place for sadness in their kingdom. One night, Jonny's mother heard a child crying. The cries came from the edge of the woods. The whole family awoke and ran to where the cries came from. They found Jonny sitting under a tree. He was hugging a large Teddy bear. The whole village celebrated Jonny's return.

# CHAPTER 5

## Lazy Joe

Grandma and her grandchildren were coming home from the park on her fourth day with them. Jasmine just started to drive the SUV when Olivia screamed. "Brian is left behind!" Grandma who was sitting with Jasmine in the front was horrified. "Let's go back to the park, quick!" They found Brian with a group of older boys. They were teasing him. One grabbed the boy and was pushing him to the ground.

"Stop it! You!" Grandma confronted the bully, holding his arm. Brian was crying. He told his story when they were back in their vehicle. "They wanted me to join them go to the woods. They dared who got the most and best strawberries. I refused to go with them. I am scared of the fairies!" "There, there, don't be afraid. Grandma would never let the fairies take you."

During bedtime, grandma told her grandchildren: "My story tonight is not about fairies. It is about the laziest boy in the village. His name was

Joe, and the title of my story is "Lazy Joe." Would

you like to hear this story or would you prefer a story

about enchanted beings?"

"Yes, Yes, grandma! I like to hear more about

fairies and enchanted castles!" Olivia enthusiastically

exclaimed. "No! No! No!" Brian almost screamed,

covering himself with a blanket. "All right children,

let's have a compromise. Let's have the Lazy Joe story

tonight, and tomorrow, I shall tell another story about

princes and castles, which Olivia likes."

"Joe was 10 years old. He was a very lazy boy,

so lazy that anything his mother would tell him to

do, he refused to do, or if he did it, he never did the

right thing. Worst, he did it without caring for the result of what he had done wrong. His parents could not understand the boy. In school, his teacher would often make him stand in front of the class or keep him inside the classroom during recess time. The teacher's complaints reached his parents. They finally took him out of school out of frustration.

These were few of lazy Joe's misdeeds: One day, his mother sent him to the village open market to buy a couple of earthen jars. The jars were made of earth mixed with water, molded and dried. The mother intended them for storing salted fish. John lifted one jar and decided it was heavy for him to carry. He took a small bamboo pole, made a hole through each jar and inserted the pole through them. Now, he could carry them with more ease. He smiled thinking of his cleverness. His mother almost beat him up when he got home with the jars having holes in them, but he ran away. It was the middle of the day and the bright sun hit him. He rested under a mango tree laden with ripe fruits. Soon, he was fast asleep. When he woke up much later, he felt very hungry. The ripe mangos above him looked very tempting. He wished they would fall! He was so lazy that he did not want to rise and climb the tree to get the luscious fruits. So he waited for the ripe mangos to fall. He positioned himself underneath a laden branch and waited for the

birds to come. He opened his mouth so that the fruit

would fall directly into it. The birds came all right,

but they took away all the ripe mangos. Lazy Joe was

left very hungry, but still he continued to wait for the

birds to come to pluck the mangos for him. None of

the birds came again. Poor Joe!

# CHAPTER 6

## Lazy Joe and the Chickens

Saturday was a market day in Joe's small town. His mother sent him to the market early in the afternoon to buy live chickens for their dinner. The vendor put out all her live chickens for Joe to choose from. He chose two biggest chickens from the rest. The woman vendor tied up the live fowls and handed them over to the boy. "Enjoy your dinner, son. I'm sure your mother will cook a very delicious chicken dinner tonight," the woman said to him smiling.

Joe thought of something to relieve him the burden of carrying the chickens home. They were heavy and were restless being tied up together and put in a basket. He sat down at the side of the road and untied the chickens. "Go on home. You would be happy without being tied up. Come on, walk home," John ordered." Of course the fowls did not know any better. "Hurry! "You two! Joe pushed and shouted at the chickens, threatening to beat them up.

Fed up that the chickens were very slow walking, he demanded," You are too slow for me. I'll walk ahead of you. I'll see the two of you at home." He then

sauntered ahead of the chickens, whistling as he went.

When he got home, his mother asked, "Where are

the chickens?" They are coming, mother. They walk

slowly, so I gave them a little time." The mother was

so indignant he chased John all over the house with a

big stick in hand."You stupid fool! You will not have

supper tonight!"

## Lazy Joe and His Uncle

Joe's uncle David was a fisherman. One day, he

took Joe with him to go fishing. They were way up

the middle of the ocean when it started to rain hard.

Soon the wind blew fiercely, rocking their boat from side to side. The rocking of the boat made Joe drowsy, so he fell asleep in the midst of the raging storm.

"Joe, Joe," his uncle shouted. Get the spare oar and help me row!" But Joe was fast asleep. Just then a huge wave swept their hapless boat and threw both of them out of the boat. Joe's uncle was able to cling to the side of the capsized boat, but Joe disappeared into the ocean, still asleep. When he woke up, it was very dark and he was choking. He felt around him. Everything he touched was wet and soft. He began to shiver in the cold of the chamber he did not know what. "Where am I? Help! Help!" No one answered

his frantic cries for help.

Joe began to panic. Whatever place he was in

was certainly not a good one."Am I inside a cave? A

tunnel? But they don't move. This one kept moving

and moving zigzag, as if it was a submarine? Were

submarines wet and cold inside? He asked himself.

"Help! Please help me!" He screamed aloud, beating

the walls of his prison furiously with his fists. He

repeated screaming and pounding on the wet walls

until he could not utter any sound no more. Suddenly,

he heard a loud roar, then a laugh. "You fool, you will

remain inside me until you learn to be useful. You

have been so lazy you deserve to be punished." "Who

are you? Where am I?" Ah! You want to know me

and where you are right now? Well, dumb boy, I am

a whale and I swallowed you into my belly. I think I

won't be hungry for awhile now." "Please release me.

I want to go home. I promise to be good and not to

be lazy again." The whale spat Joe out on the beach

with a warning."Watch out boy, if you don't keep your

promise, you will be in trouble again."

"Grandma, grandma, did Lazy Joe keep his promise?" Olivia shook grandma's arm when the latter paused. "Oh, yes. Joe might be lazy and dumb, but he knew that promises should be kept. Besides, he was terrified that the whale might swallow him up again. I have another story about Joe as a changed boy. First, let me give you a scoop of ice cream each, then get ready for my next story." "Yeah!" Brian exclaimed enthusiastically. Two scoops please, grandma." Grandma went to the refrigerator then came back with two scoops of ice cream for both her grandchildren.

# CHAPTER 7

## Joe the Hero

From a skinny, freckled lad of 10, Joe grew to be a tall and strong 16 year-old teen. He could pitch in their school's baseball team so well that his team won almost all the games. He could also fish as good as his father. He would always come home from fishing with his father or with his friends with a good catch. He was handy in all the household tasks. While his two younger sisters played, he would tinker in his father's work bench, or help his mother with household chores. He was very trustworthy and reliable. He never took any extra allowance and whatever amount left every end of the week, he would tell his mother and father that they could give him lesser amount since he still had leftover money. He was such a good teenager that his parents openly praised him to their neighbors and friends. He was also generally liked by his classmates and was his teachers' favorite.

One day, while Joe and his school mates went on a field trip to the cotton field a mile from their school, one of his school mates, a girl of 14 disappeared. They searched the entire area the whole day until night but the girl was nowhere to be found. The town police were summoned and search parties were organized. They searched the entire cotton field, two acres in area and the outlying fields but the girl could not be found.

They gave up after four days search. The police posted a missing person sign with the girl's picture on it and circulated them around the township and in neighboring districts. The parents of the girl were inconsolable. It was generally believed that the girl was abducted. There was another abduction in the township a few months back. The boy of 8 was found dead, buried under thick dry leaves near the creek three miles from home. The case was still under investigation.

Joe was among the diligent searchers of the missing girl. Each time he would see the girl's mother weeping, he would nearly shed a tear himself. It must be awful to lose a family member. He could not imagine losing any of his family. It would probably kill him with grief. So, whenever his sisters went out to play, he was always there watching them. In school, he made it a point to wait for them or ask them to wait up for him when he had a game.

On the fifth day of the girl's disappearance, Joe ventured alone into the cotton fields. He did not really expect anything, but he was filled with hope that somehow, he would find something, even just a tiny clue to what happened to the girl, Gisela. At midday, he became weary from the heat of the noonday sun. He sat under a maple tree at the edge of the cotton field, and soon he was fast asleep, fanned by the gentle breeze.

It was late in the afternoon when he awoke from some kind of muffled sound. Half asleep, he could hear a faint thumping from beneath the tree, or so it seemed. He listened again, now fully awake. The sound came again and this time, he determined that it came from under the tree. Was it a squirrel? Or a mouse trapped under the dry leaves?

Joe sprang to his feet and began clawing at the thick dry maple leaves around the tree. He clawed and dug fiercely. The sound came more vividly now. It sounded like a low sobbing. John stopped at his right hand side where the sobbing emanated from, and concentrated on the spot. Then, he saw a hole, as big as a well's hole. It was shallow, possibly filled with sand, pebbles and leaves. Then a girl's head appeared from under the thick dry leaves that covered the hole.

Joe lay down on his stomach and reached out to the girl who was now staring at him with mournful eyes. She looked badly hurt. He could not reach the girl's hand. He said to the girl in a comforting voice, "Gisela?" The girl only nodded weakly."Try to reach out to my hand." The girl tried, but she was too weak to even put up her hand. Joe thought of going down the hole, but what if the bottom of leaves and dirt would collapse under the weight of two children?

Joe looked around the place for anything he could use to bring out the girl, but he could not find anything suitable. He dug up a small canal on the surface of the hole near the girl, then he lowered his two feet with both his hands clinging to the surface

of the canal he had dug up to keep him from falling

down. Next, he asked the girl to hold on to his

dangling feet. But the girl did not make any sound.

Joe became frantic. Did the girl die? "Lord please

keep her alive," he prayed aloud, something he had

never done before. He kept on calling the girl's name,

hoping that she just passed out. Nothing. Just then, he

heard a distant sound of a car engine. He rose quickly

and ran to the road along the cotton field about 500

yards from the maple tree. Joe ran faster than he had

ever ran before, screaming for help as he went. The

pickup truck stopped as it was about to turn a bend.

Joe rapidly told his story and the two men abandoned their vehicle. The three of them went running to the spot where Joe had left the girl.

The other guy ran back to the pick-up truck and took a ladder. As he was lighter than any of the two men, Joe volunteered to go down the ladder. The leaves and soft earth were now showing signs of giving in. He quickly hoisted the girl up into the hands of the two men with care. The girl was still breathing but faintly. She was bruised all over and had an ugly gash on her forehead. The loss of blood, hunger and thirst weakened her and made her unconscious.

When she was well again under the care of the doctor and her doting parents, she told her story. She decided to make a prank during the field trip. She went ahead of the group and climbed the tree, crouching on the biggest branch. She had meant to join her group when no one seemed to have noticed her disappearance, but when she jumped to the ground, she fell into the hole. The thick leaves and pebbles covered her unconscious body. She did not know how long she had been unconscious. When she came to, it was very quiet and dark. She was screaming and screaming until she could not utter even a whimper. Nobody seemed to hear her.

She was alternating between consciousness and unconsciousness. She chewed on the moist leaves. They quenched some of her thirst and silenced her grumbling stomach. When Joe found her, she was conscious but drifted into unconsciousness again.

Joe became the township hero and an instant celebrity. The town mayor awarded him a medal of courage and the school recommended him full scholarship. The parents of the girl offered him a tidy sum but he declined. He declared wisely, that his reward was to have done his best under the circumstances. What he had done offered him the greatest satisfaction more than any reward could give.

"Grandma, I would like to be a hero one day." Brian declared solemnly. "How could you be a hero, Brian? You are scared even with a tiny, harmless mouse. You have to be brave to be a hero." Olivia said wisely. "Your sister is right, my boy." Grandma put in. "You could be a hero, Brian when you grow up. You are scared easily now since you are still small. When you grow up, you will be a hero if you strive to be." Brian gave grandma his hard to come by sweet smile.

Grandma and her grandchildren spent part of one evening singing. She sang two songs, which the kids liked. Brian even asked her to sing them again. Her first song was a longtime favorite, a song popularized in the 50's, entitled "Today." She sang the same song to a big crowd of tourists at a huge open air auditorium in Ceasaria, Israel during one of her cruises. Their tour guide asked the tourist passengers who wanted to sing. As there was nobody who wanted to sing, grandma volunteered. She had thought that she was to sing in the bus on the way to Ceasaria, but the guide did not mention it again until they arrived in Ceasaria. She took grandma to the middle of the stage and prodded on her to "give it her best."

Grandma was taken by surprise with this unexpected assignment, to sing to a large, unfamiliar crowd of tourists from all over the world. It was a real challenge. Grandma liked challenges and surprises, so she boldly sang to her expectant audience. A loud applause followed her impromptu performance. Grandma could never forget that day when she became an instant international celebrity. When Olivia heard her story, she prevailed on her grandmother to sing the song to them again. Following is the memorable song: "Today:"

"Today while the blossoms still cling to the vine; I'll taste your strawberries and drink your sweet wine. A million tomorrows shall all pass away, then I'll forget all the joys that are mine today.

Refrain: I'll be a dandy and I'll be a rover, you know who I am by the song that I sing, Today is my moment and now is my glory who cares what tomorrow shall be.{Repeat first stanza) The other song that grandma sang to the children was entitled "Mocking Bird Hill.""

"When the sun in the morning peeps over the hill and kisses the roses round my window sill. Then my heart's full of gladness whenever I hear all the birds on the treetops on the mocking Bird Hill. Tra la la, twiddle dee dee it gives me a thrill to wake up in the morning on the Mocking Bird hill.(Repeat) When it's late in the morning I climb up the hill and survey the meadow down Mocking Bird hill, then my heart's full of gladness as I go down the hill of beauty and peace on the Mocking Bird Hill." The children clapped loudly at the end of each song.

Olivia liked the first song, but Brian insisted that he preferred the second song. Grandma sang both songs again, then again when she put her grandkids to bed. The rest of the evening was spent singing and then dancing by Olivia. Brian was too shy to do anything except fencing, which grandma was obliged to do with him. It was a fun evening.

# CHAPTER 8

# The Prince Who Became a Frog

In a far, foreign country, there lived an old monarch, King Sebastian and his wife, Queen Sheena. They had two sons, Ranon, 16 and his younger brother Dino, 14 years old. The Golden Kingdom, so called because it was made with precious gold was not only magical but also formidable. It was heavily protected with high double walls around its wide, sprawling grounds, planted with green, well-trimmed grass and bordered with hundreds of different types of flowers. Well-armed guards were stationed outside, inside the entrance and all around the palace grounds. In spite of its opulence and grandeur, the kingdom had never been robbed or attacked by marauders.

Perhaps the reason for the peace and security the kingdom enjoyed was not due to its heavy fortifications, but due to the kindness, generosity and popularity of the king and the queen. They befriended all the other kingdoms in the country and gave generously to neighbors and to the poor near or far, and especially to their soldiers and subjects. The kingdom prospered steadily through the years and it earned another name

to its crown, the "Golden Haven."

The two princes were nurtured in the most

loving and caring environment. At an early age, they

each had two governesses. One governess saw to their

physical needs and welfare, while the other to their

moral and spiritual upbringing. The royal couple

was very happy and proud of their two boys. Life

in the golden palace was like a fairytale, no sorrow,

no fear and want, only fun, merriment and general

contentment. However, one day, when Prince Dino

was fifteen years old, things became marred by the

boy's sudden change of behavior. He became unruly

and disobedient, even disrespecting the King and taunting the Queen mother. The royal couple and the entire royal household believed this change was caused by the prince' coming of age. Some teenagers, royal or subjects were known to change not only in their physical make up but also in their behavior. They did not take so much notice until one day when Prince Dino disappeared.

A thorough search within the palace was conducted. They hoped that this was just a boy's prank. Night and day, the search continued but there was no trace of the boy. King Sebastian himself went with a search party outside the palace and beyond. He enlisted the other kingdoms to help in searching for the boy, but all efforts were in vain. King Sebastian and Queen Sheena were inconsolable. The once glittering and happy kingdom turned into a gloomy palace.

Meanwhile, Prince Dino wandered in the forest alone, searching for something he did not even know what. He hid in the bushes and behind boulders to escape from his searchers. He was happy with his freedom and he was determined to enjoy it for as long as he could. He had longed to discover the outside world and now, nothing could stop him, not even his loving parents. Surely, there were numerous things that need knowing and discovering on his own. His governesses had taught him a lot of things but his appetite for new things was insatiable.

Prince Dino continued his trek into the forest, stopping only to eat wild berries and other wild fruits. Resting on the banks of a deep river, he saw an unusually large frog. It was so large that Dino thought it was a human sitting on the stone. "Hello, Prince Dino, can you help me catch some fish? I am very hungry. I have been trying to catch one since early this morning, but no luck." "What? So you can speak? Let me see. I should like to test your language ability. You say, "Oh, Prince Dino. You are the most handsome prince I ever saw. I will serve you until I die."

The frog hesitated, then said. "I can't say that, bad prince. To die for you is the last thing I would do in my lifetime! However, if you promise to change your bad ways, I will give you this whole forest, this river, the hills and the mountain, and everything else besides." "Liar! And how dare you defy me!" Dino screamed. You are but an ugly, miserable frog!" He took a knife from his waist and hit the frog on the chest. The frog fell into the water, dying.

Before the frog gave his last breath, he cursed the boy. "Because of your evil deed, I will turn you into a frog like me. You will only get back to being a human again if an innocent, beautiful girl hugs and kisses you." With these words, the dying frog sank into the deepest part of the river. Dino laughed aloud and said mockingly. "Impertinent, useless creature! Who are you to say such nonsense? I am invincible and cannot be touched by any curse." He left the river and headed back to the palace.

It was growing dark. Darkness descended faster in the deserted, thick forest. Dino started to worry that he might not be able to reach the palace before it got very dark. While Dino was walking, he felt very, very tired. He kept on walking until he could no longer lift his feet. He collapsed under a huge tree, whose branches were hanging low. A small river flowed alongside it.

His fatigue overcame him and soon, he fell into a deep sleep under the tree's huge trunk. He dreamed of the large frog which he had just killed. It was alive and was pointing a finger at him. "Sleep on, wicked prince, sleep on and wake up tomorrow in a different world." It laughed so loud that the tree shook.

Dino woke up late the following morning. He stretched and yawned. Why couldn't he hear himself yawning? And why wouldn't his legs stretch? He looked down at his body. He could not see his body. What he saw was a brown, slimy form, slippery limbs and thin, long legs! He touched his head, his face, neck and his mouth. He felt a small, rough face with a large mouth. Where was his neck? And what happened to his whole body? He ran to the river and looked at his reflection in the clear water. He was a frog, a large, ugly frog!

Dino was beside himself with unusual apprehension and worry, emotions he had never experienced before. So the frog was telling the truth. His cursed on him worked! What to do now? What could a frog do? He leapt and jumped here and there, hoping to shake off his new form, to no avail. He broke down. Had he ever cried before? No. He had no reason to. Even when his older brother hit him for being so naughty, he never cried. He hit Ranon back real hard, so hard the latter cried in pain. Ranon was always the crying baby. On the other hand, he was strong, brave and never let anyone made him cry.

How would he get back to the enchanted frog who turned him into this miserable state? He would crush it with a stone and throw the pieces into the river. Its current should reduce it to nothing, he vowed.

After days of hopping and limping, he could now see the palace tower high above the trees. It was shrouded by low hanging clouds. It was a cloudy, dreary day. It reflected the somber mood inside the palace. Dino's grieving parents had given up hope to see their son alive. It had been several days that their hunt for the missing boy had been abandoned.

The fortune teller they had consulted said that Dino

was captured by bad fairies and held captive in their

underworld abode. There was no way to rescue him.

Dino decided to get a long rest on a big stone

lying along the road on the way to the well-guarded

palace. What if the guards would see him and kill

him? It was impossible not to get noticed by the overly

watchful guards in his present state. One sweep of a

guard's sword would kill him instantly. He grimaced.

While he was contemplating his next move, two boys

passed by. He was not quick enough to hide behind

the stone. They pelted him with pebbles. One pebble

hit him slightly on his belly. He fell from the stone.

The boys left him thinking maybe that he was dead.

While he was nursing his hurt belly, three soldiers came by and stopped. They dismounted from their horses and allowed the animals to drink from the river. Then, they rested on a log and slept. Dino thought of doing a prank, a habit he always enjoyed doing. He crawled slowly, noiselessly approached a soldier and tickled his ear. The soldier awoke, startled. He cursed under his breath and caught Dino with one hand. But the slippery frog prince somehow slipped from the soldier's grasp and jumped away into the other side of the bank. The soldier took a bow and arrow and aimed at the frog prince. The arrow almost hit him! A fallen branch took the tip of the arrow, missing the frog prince for only an inch.

A boy on a pony and an older man were walking along the path close by. Dino was fascinated with the white pony the boy was riding on. It looked so much like his pony back in the palace grounds. As he came out closer to watch the pony walk by, the boy spotted him. He led the pony where Dino was and was at the point of trampling on him if Dino was not quick enough to escape. What horrible attempts on his life! Was there no end to the dangers he was facing? The frog prince decided to lie low for awhile as he pondered on the possibilities ahead of him.

In his hideout, Dino began to feel sorry for himself. He wondered if animals ever felt sorry for their state of helplessness against humans. Oh, that he could go back to his human form! He was in a state of hopelessness when he heard a girl's sobbing. It came from the woods nearby. Dino became curious. Why would a girl wander into the woods alone? Was she lost? He peered from behind the bush he was hiding. The girl continued to wail. Dino took pity on the miserable girl. He slowly, carefully came out of his hiding place. Surely, this young creature was harmless. He convinced himself. He thought of doing something that would make the girl stop crying. Like what? What could a worthless frog do in this situation?

Of course, croak! He laughed to himself. Was this not the way frogs communicate with each other? But with humans, will it work? With all his strength, he croaked as loud and as melodious as he could. He waited, then croaked again as he just did. Did she hear him? The girl suddenly stopped crying and turned her head in his direction. There was a hint of delight in her dirty face. She wiped away the tears from her eyes with her arm and stooped in front of him.

"Oh, you poor thing! Can you be my friend? I am so lonely. My name is Cita. I would like to go home but I do not know the way. My friends left me picking wild berries. Can you take me home, please?" The frog prince almost leapt with joy. His heart felt not only pity for the girl, but a desire to help her get home. The girl put out her two hands and scooped him. Next, she held him close to her, brushed her cheek on his slimy body and gave him a quick kiss.

Suddenly, A cloud covered the area around the prince frog and the girl. Then, a tender voice could be heard behind the cloud."Prince Dino, since you have felt pity and has the intention of helping a helpless girl, you are now free of your bondage, on one condition.

When you arrive back to your palace, take the girl on a carriage to her family. Help the girl's village from extreme poverty. One day when you grow up, take the girl as your wife." When the voice ceased, the cloud lifted and revealed a boy of sixteen in his full royal regalia.

Dino followed the voice' advise and married the girl after his 18th birthday. They inherited the Golden Kingdom after King Sebastian and Queen Sheena died. His older brother, Ranon married a princess in another kingdom. King Dino and Princess Cita lived happily ever after.

Grandma was a little surprised to see her grandchildren fully awake throughout her long story. Brian, lying on her lap sat up and said seriously. "Grandma, is there a way I can be a prince one day?

"Brian, don't be silly. How can you be a prince? You have to be a son of a king and queen to become a prince." Olivia said to his brother, laughing.

"I think you can be a prince, my dear boy." Grandma said as seriously. Tomorrow, we shall go to the Medieval Store and get a prince' outfit. What about you, Olivia, dear? Would you like to be a princess? We can get a princess' dress also. Then, tomorrow evening after supper, we shall play a royal march around the living room, and take pictures in

your royal outfit for mom." "Yes, Yes, grandma. Let's

do that!" The children exclaimed at the same time,

hugging their grandmother.

# CHAPTER 9

## The Three Orphans

On the fifth night of grandma's babysitting, she was checking the children's homework before dinner, a daily routine for her since she came. "Come here, Olivia, sweetie. Two of your words in this composition are incorrectly spelled. Let's correct it." "Grandma, look at my drawings. My teacher in kindergarten said I could draw very well. Do you like this one?" Brian showed his drawing of a forest, with wild flowers bordering it. "Wow! Wonderful! I think this is better than what you did yesterday and the other day. Let me see your writing exercise book. Brian, my boy, let me help you improve your handwriting. Your S and your G are a bit awkward. Here, let me show you."

After dinner when the kitchen had been cleared up, grandma followed the children to the family room. "Let's wait for mommy's call. She said yesterday that she would be a little late in calling tonight because a special guest at the conference is going to speak. It could take long. Meanwhile let me tell a story about three orphan children."

In a little town a mile from the railroad tracks, Vicky, 10, Selena, 8 and Toby, 5 years old, lived with their aunt Helena and her husband Victor with two of their children, 6 and 11 years old. The three children's parents died in a car crash a few months back. They had no other relatives, so the burden of rearing the orphans fell into the aunt and uncle's shoulders. The Childrens' Home in the city was full. Besides, Helena did not want her nieces and nephew to live in a crowded public facility.

Helena was very kind to the children, but her husband was a different story. He was cruel and abusive. When he got home from work, he would ask them not to make any noise while he was taking

a nap. If anyone of the kids made even the slightest

giggle, talking, closing or opening doors, etc., he

maltreated her/him. One afternoon, while Victor was

napping, Toby dropped a fork on the wooden floor

in the kitchen. It made a small, ringing sound. Victor

marched into the kitchen and kicked the boy in the

butt.

Vicky was not fast enough in handing Victor

the hoe while they were gardening. He hit her leg with

the hoe. It swelled for awhile. Vicky hardly got over

her bruise, when Victor slapped her for her failure to

iron his shirt. Selena was usually quiet and kept to

herself away from the abusive man. One day, Selena

did not hear her uncle calling her from his workshop.

He was repairing a bike. At the third call, the man

strode angrily into the children's bedroom, dragged

the girl outside and twisted her ears. "Are you deaf?

Here, take this to make you hear!

Once, their aunt Helena intervened when Victor

did not want the children to eat with them at the

dining table. He wanted them to eat in the kitchen.

The couple had a shouting match, which ended in

the wife's beating. After two more incidents of wife

beating, Helena cautioned the children to be extra

careful not to cross the ill-tempered man. Whenever

the husband was around in the house, Helena would send the children for errands in town, or to some place else to avoid her abusive husband. Stopping him or intervening only made things worse for her.

One Saturday morning, when Victor came home early from a ballgame with his children, Helena urged his nieces and nephew to go to the open market to buy jams, bread and milk. The three orphans did not come back home. Helena was filled with worry for her nieces and nephew. She was restless and could not sleep the whole night. The husband did not show any concern for the children. In fact, he did not mind at all if they never came back. Meanwhile, the children headed to the outskirts of the town, avoiding the main roads. They did not want to be seen by anyone. They followed the old railway tracks that were no longer used. When they got hungry, they picked berries along the way and drank from the creek. They walked all day long not knowing where they were heading. They only rested for a while when Toby was too tired to continue. The hot sun made them all exhausted but they went on their aimless trek. They wanted to cover as far away from home as they could.

They were crossing the train tracks when two

ferocious dogs appeared from nowhere, baring their

teeth and barking at them. The poor, tired kids

managed to climb a tree nearby. Vicky was almost

caught by one of the dogs when she hoisted his brother

up before she climbed after him. Selena almost fell

from a weak branch but caught another larger and

stronger branch on time. Bruised, clothes tattered and weary, the terrified children remained on their perch long after the animals had left.

Late in the afternoon, they came to a big clearing. They saw large crowds of people dancing and children playing. Loud music from guitars and drums dominated the whole place. There was a carousel in the middle of the clearing. The children became curious. They decided to stop and see what was going on. On the arched entrance, a big sign said: "Country Fair, Welcome Guests! Welcome All!" Holding each other's hands, they went inside and headed to the food booths. They were very hungry and tired. Maybe someone would be kind enough to give them some food, or maybe a place to rest? But before they reached the food booth, a group of mean boys came.

The children wanted to run away but the mean boys surrounded them. Hi! Vagabonds! The biggest and possibly the oldest in the group shouted at them. "You have no right to be here. You are filthy and ugly! Which garbage dump did you come from?" They ridiculed the children and started to break them from each other's hold. The children fought hard. Vicky hit the bigger boy on the shoulder when he started to tear off her clothes. Two smaller boys grabbed Toby and held him down on the ground. Selena picked up a stone and struck a boy's knees hard when he pulled her long hair, making him scream in pain.

The fight was still going on when a carriage arrived in the fair grounds. A uniformed man approached and said. "What's going on here? Why are you fighting?" The children wept, clinging to each other. In a trembling voice, Vicky told their story. "They just attacked us. We did not come here to cause trouble." Tearfully, Selena said in a very low voice," We only wanted to get something to eat. We did not eat the whole day."

A middle aged couple joined them shortly. They were dressed in expensive clothes and looked very distinguished. Seeing the miserable looking children huddled together on the ground, the lady asked. "Pray, what's the matter here? Why are these poor children weeping, Armand? Who are these children? They look so pitiful." The lady stooped, took Toby's dirty hands and lifted him up. Next, she held Selena's arm and helped her stand. Her husband helped Vicky rise and brushed away the dirt from her skirt.

"Armand, tell Reynaldo to get the car and bring these children to the hotel. Also, tell him to ask the maid to give them shower, clean clothes and food. We shall join them later after our dinner with the Mayor.

The kind couple learned about the children's sad plight when they got back to their hotel. Vicky told them about losing their mother and father and having been habitually abused by their aunt's husband. They ran away and would not want to go back.

When they were alone together in their bedroom, Lady Mathilde said to her husband. "Clod, I pity these children very much. How about if we adopt them? Our only child, Dotty would be happy with them, don't you think?" Very good idea, dear. I like them. They seem very well behaved." "I like them a lot too. They would make good companions to our little Dotty."

The following day, the last day of the couple's stay in town, Mathilde's sister, Rowena arrived from London unexpectedly. She said she was bored waiting for her sister and wanted to spend some time in the countryside as well. She was childless and a widow of five years. When she saw the three children, she was very delighted. "Mathilde, I should like to be the one to adopt these children, please. I have always wanted to adopt children as you know. Besides, you already have one child, but I have none."

"What about if I get one of them and you the other two?" Mathilde suggested. When they told the children about their plan, they appeared very happy. However, Vicky did not want them separated. "Sorry, madam Mathilde and madam Rowena, but we need to be together in one place. My sister, my brother and I have never been separated before." She embraced Selena and Toby. The children hugged each other. It was a touching scene.

A compromise was reached. The three children would live with Rowena in her London suburb mansion. Mathilde and her husband would have them during the weekends. The sisters lived only a block away from each other. The children could not be more happy in their new-found, affluent abode. They found the ideal parents they never had.

"Children, did you like the story I just told you?" Grandma noticed Brian dosing off. "I guess Brian got bored. There was not much excitement in that story but my next one, hopefully, will interest you more." "I love the story, grandma," Olivia said, yawning. Just then, the telephone rang. It was now almost 10:00 p.m. Angela came on the wire anxiously. "Mom, sorry to call you this late. The conference took so long tonight. Are the children still awake?" "Oh, yes. They have been waiting for your call." Grandma

took the other phone from the next room so that both

her grandchildren could listen to their mom at the

same time.

# CHAPTER 10

## Loro, the Parrot

Next evening, grandma allowed the children to finish watching a movie during dinner, entitled "Hachi," a story about a Japanese dog who escaped from his cage when its handler just arrived on an airline in the U.S. from Japan. A professor, played by Richard Gere found him and adopted him. It was a moving story of a dog so attached with his master that even after he died, the faithful dog continued to meet his train at the station. Every day, Hachi would sit at his usual place and wait for his master at the station at the usual time it arrived every day, until when the dog died of old age. The children enjoyed the movie very much. Grandma wept silently seeing the last scene when the dog was found dead. She missed her two dogs, Tinsel and Buddy.

"Olivia, Brian, if you are interested to hear my story tonight, finish up your dinner. You will have ice cream for dessert only if you eat a slice of pear or apple first." "I do not like pear or apple, grandma. Can I have half a banana?" You already had banana this morning, sweetheart. What about melon slices?" "I want melon, too, grandma." Olivia said, getting two small bowls from the cupboard. Grandma cleared up the kitchen while the children ate their fruit.

"I'll be waiting in the family room when you are done." When the children joined her, grandma sat between them and said. "Day after tomorrow, your mom will be coming home. I'll have two more stories for you after tonight." I'll be going back home the day after your mom's arrival." "You are leaving us grandma? Why don't you stay with us?" Olivia asked, clutching grandma's arm. Brian did not say anything. He just gazed at grandma with sadness in his eyes.

"I wish I could, but I miss my two dogs. I can't be away from them too long. The dog sitter has to go somewhere and expects me to be back on Monday. Don't worry. Your mom said she is going to attend another conference in Chicago a couple of months from now. And you know what? She is going to take you both with her. You are going to visit me and your aunt Bing and uncle Ariel in Huntley when the conference is over. "Yeah, Yeah, Yeah!" Olivia and Brian jumped excitedly. "Now, for our story. Settle down, my darlings."

The Lawrence family was having breakfast one early morning when they heard a squeaking sound coming from their backyard. It was sharp, and sounded like "Hello! Hello!" Curious, the two young children, Zenny and Raul ran to the back door. The sound became louder and more distinct as the children approached. "Hi! Hi!" The greeting continued. They saw a large parrot perched on their wooden fence!

"Mommy, daddy, look! You won't believe what's here!" The children cried excitedly. Their parents left the breakfast table and joined their children. "Hi! There!" The parrot went on its greetings. "Amazing! A talking parrot? I have never seen or heard one before." The husband said unbelievingly. I have heard of them but never saw one before," the wife remarked, moving

closer to the bird. It did not fly away as she thought

it would.

"Hello, yourself! Where do you come from?

Do you have a name?" Loro, my name is Loro." The

parrot spoke clearly. It was not scared of them at all.

In fact, it was very tame and friendly. The family

came closer to the bird. Mr. Lawrence touched his

feather gently and said. "Let me introduce my family.

Now, where did you come from? Did you fly away

from your previous owner? Why?" The parrot was

silent for a while. Then it flapped its wings. They

thought it was going to fly away, but it only moved to the corner of the fence.

Finally, it said. "I would like to stay with you. I don't belong to anyone. Can I stay?" "Of course, you can. We welcome you with us!" The family was delighted. They each took turns in petting the talking bird. Mr. Lawrence went to the pet store and got food and a cage for Loro. During the day, they allowed him to stay around the house. At night, he was put inside the cage.

One night, a strong storm came. It ripped part of their garage roof. Loro was restless. When the family was sleeping, they awoke from Loro's loud scream.

"Basement! Water in basement! Flood! Mr. Lawrence

got up and rushed to the basement. It was flooded!

When he looked outside, their street was flooded

too. Debris from higher ground was floating on the

flooded street and the water rose steadily. Their house

was now flooding inside too. "Quick! Everyone, get

to the attic!" Mr. and Mrs. Lawrence gathered their

blankets and herded the children upstairs.

"Wait, wait for me," Loro pleaded. In their

state of anxiety, they forgot about the bird. Mr.

Lawrence waded in knee deep water and took Loro

out from his cage. The Lawrence family endured

their cramped attic room throughout the night.

Luckily, the storm subsided in the morning hours.

They thanked Loro for waking them up just in time to escape the flood waters inside the house.

Burglary was common in their neighborhood but the Lawrence family was not concerned. They were poor and only depended on Mr. Lawrence' salary every month as carpenter in a construction company. They did not have valuables to attract burglars. However, they just bought a television set last Christmas, a present for their children. Mrs. Lawrence also had a slightly used computer, which her cousin sold to her at a minimal price. The TV set and the computer were for them, treasures.

One late Sunday afternoon, the couple was out shopping for food, as was their routine every Sunday. Only the two children were home, playing in the yard. Suddenly, they heard a big commotion and shrieks from inside the house. Then, they saw two men running away from the house. They dropped the computer and the television set as they ran away. "Burglars! Call police, quick!" Loro squeaked, catching up with one of the two burglars. He picked hard on the man's bald head. The two children were beside themselves with amusement as they described the parrot's deed. Mr. and Mrs. Lawrence could not thank Loro enough. Mrs. Lawrence held him tenderly and kissed his head.

Mr. Lawrence would not fail to purchase lotto tickets every month after he cashed his paycheck. It was a habit that he could not stop. He would give his wife his whole month's salary and kept only two dollars for lotto tickets. Once, he won two hundred dollars when his second child was just a baby. It never happened again after that, but the man continued to be hopeful.

Before Mr. Lawrence left for the variety store in town where he would normally buy his tickets one late afternoon, Loro became restless in his cage.

He was flapping his wings vigorously and made loud squeaking sounds. 'Wait, Wait!" "What's the matter, Loro?" He asked the excited bird. "Out! Take me out!" "But it is now time for you to sleep." "Later, later." Loro insisted.

Loro asked Mr. Lawrence to take him to the calendar hanging on the bedroom door."Pen, paper, get." Bewildered, Mr. Lawrence did as the parrot told him. "Write numbers." With Loro on his shoulders, Mr. Lawrence wrote the numbers as the bird pointed them with his beak. When he had finished, the bird asked to be put back inside the cage. "Goodluck, Goodbye! sir!" Mr. Lawrence hurriedly left in his car, anxious to try his luck with the lotto. He picked the numbers given by Loro. Late that night, when the winning numbers were announced on the television, the whole family was on edge. Even Mrs. Lawrence who was already in bed got up and joined her family. One, two, three, four five, etc. numbers were called and appeared on the screen, but they were completely different from what Loro had given to Mr. Lawrence. The family was very disappointed.

The following morning, the winning numbers were printed on the front page of the local paper. There appeared to be no winners for the two million jackpot. With some reluctance, Mr. Lawrence compared his ticket to the printed numbers. For some reason, he

had kept it inside his coat pocket. He would normally

throw it into the waste basket after the drawing.

Boy! He was overjoyed that he did not! His numbers

matched the winning numbers! How did it happen?

Were they not different from last night's announced

winning tickets? He read on. The bold note below

the numbers said that there had been a mistake in

the television announcement. The lotto organizers

apologized for the error.

The whole family was overwhelmed with joy.

Loud flapping of bird wings interrupted the family's

jubilation. "Wow! Wow! Congratulations!" Loro was

as happy as the Lawrence family, dancing around like a delighted child. Mr. Lawrence took the bird from his perch on top of the cupboard, held him tenderly and whispered," Loro, I cannot find words to thank you, dear." His wife and children took turns in holding Loro and kissing him.

The following day, Mr. Lawrence and his family trooped inside the store to claim his winnings. They were to receive full payment as soon as the processing was done. A local reporter was called but Mr. Lawrence declined to have his name advertized. When they finally received the prize, the family made plans for their future. They were going to give up their

humble home in Orlando and move to an affluent
neighborhood in Pennsylvania. Then, Mr. Lawrence
would give up his job and invest on a restaurant
business, something he had always wanted to do.

Early one late spring morning, when Raul
approached the cage to let Loro out, he did not see
the bird. The cage was not even opened. The whole
family searched and searched but there was no sign
of their precious pet. How did it go out with the cage
tightly closed? The children were especially saddened.
Raul refused to eat. His sister, Zenny would not go
out of the room. There was a general mourning in the
household.

Mr. Lawrence took his family to the Zoo hoping to alleviate the children's sorrow. They also went to the Parrot Jungle in Miami, Florida. At the home for parrots, Mrs. Lawrence spotted a parrot inside one of the wire cages with the same size as Loro. The color of the head and beak too were like those of Loro's but it could not talk. The children were allowed to hold and play with it for some time. They wanted to take it home with them but it was not for sale, as were all the rest of the parrots. They were used for entertainment only, particularly the children. They were very tame. One could carry them on the shoulders, one on each shoulder. Raul and Zenny prevailed on their parents

for them to stay at the Parrot Jungle for a week.

The family moved to their new home in

Pennsylvania that summer. On their first night at

their elegant home, they heard flapping of wings in

the parlor. "Loro!" The family happily exclaimed in

unison. "Hello! Goodbye! I came back to say goodbye!"

Before anyone could speak, the bird flew out into the

night. They were overjoyed to see Loro although they

knew that it was the last time they would ever see their

beloved pet.

"What happened to Loro, grandma? Did he live

with another family?" Olivia asked. "Perhaps he did,

but he was not an ordinary parrot. He was probably an enchanted parrot, a creature who has abilities that we humans can neither understand or do." "I'd like to see a live parrot, grandma. Where can I see one?"" Brian said to grandma as she was handing a bowl of freshly-made popcorn. "Well, let me see. I do not see any place around here that has a parrot. The Zoo would surely have them, but it probably is far from here. I'll check in the internet and if it is not too far, we will ask Jasmine to drive us there. If it is, then let us ask mommy when she gets back. Olivia was busy reading the Encyclopedia."Here, Brian, can you draw this parrot? I'll draw it too. Let's see who does the best drawing." "Children, let's move into the study table."

You would be more comfortable doing your work

there." Grandma allowed the children to finish their

drawing until bed time. She hang their handiwork on

the refrigerator door for their mom to see.

# CHAPTER 11

## Army Buddies

Danilo and Joseph were very close friends. They had been since they were in the army during the Vietnam War. Danilo was a sergeant and Joseph was a corporal. During a raid in a Pyongyang village, Danilo was hit on the right shoulder by a sniper perched on top of a coconut tree. Joseph shot the sniper with his automatic rifle just in time before the enemy could fire a second shot. Danilo would have bled to death if Joseph had not carried him to the camp a kilometer away. His wound was superficial but he remained in camp until he was well enough to resume his duty.

The two soldiers met again during an enemy ambush in a cane field. Danilo's platoon of twenty soldiers was crossing a wide cane field to join the other regiment on the other side which needed reinforcement. They were surrounded by the enemy but luckily, through sheer luck, courage and bravery of the soldiers, Danilo's soldiers overcame them after a fierce gun battle. Danilo fell from a leg wound during the fight. Again, Joseph came to his sergeant's rescue.

He covered the wounded soldier with his body while he engaged the enemy. Only eleven soldiers came out alive with four wounded men, including Sgt. Danilo.

They were having breakfast in a well-hidden camp early one rainy morning. Suddenly, a mortar landed in the middle of the barracks. One third of the thirty men perished and five got seriously wounded. Joseph was among the severely injured. Sgt. Danilo, who was not eating with the men in the mess hall, found his friend in great agony from a wound on his right side. He rushed out in a jeep alone to the other camp across the coconut grove to get a medic, not thinking about the danger he was facing from the enemy who seemed to be everywhere.

Joseph took a long time to recover. They lacked the necessary medications and the constant movement from one place to another hampered the healing process. Sgt. Danilo was always at Joseph's side and held one end of his hammock while they navigated through marshes, swamps and hills. He comforted the sick soldier and urged him to eat whatever food they could find along the way to a bigger camp site. When Danilo went on a mission, he was strengthened and struggled to survive, thinking about his friend who needed him.

The two buddies were separated when orders of deployment came. They did not have a way to communicate with each other. They were discharged at different times, Danilo ahead of Joseph before the war was over and Joseph after the war. Danilo went home to his parents in Long Island, New York and Joseph went to live with his sister and her family in Queens, N. York.

Two years later, while Danilo was on the line for a hot meal at a Soup Kitchen in Manhattan, New York City, he felt a strong tap on his shoulders. It was his buddy, Joseph. He was the third on the line from him. They hugged each other and moved to the back of the line so that they would have a chance to talk.

"Fancy you, buddy to be here! I could hardly believe my eyes when I saw you behind me on the line!" Danilo exclaimed. "Me too! Who would have dreamed I would see my dear sergeant queuing for food?" Joseph stared at his once upon a time sergeant in the army, looking at him up and down. "Well, my friend, my life had changed dramatically since I was honorably discharged from the army." "In what sense? Good or…."Oh, I know what you were going to say next." Danilo interrupted. "It was not exactly bad for me, but only a bit unlucky. I married my girlfriend last year. We had a rough relationship. She took off with a more lucky man. Fortunately, we did not have any children. It would have been devastating for me. I could not manage my life after that unhappy union especially when my parents died in a car accident. I drifted from one place to another after my tragedies."

"What about you? Are you the luckier one?" He held his buddy's hand as they moved forward on the line. "Luckier? That's a super word to describe my situation. Sergeant, you would not see me here if I were luckier than you are. I got married too, but she died six months after our wedding. She had a lingering illness that took a bad turn. I did not want my parents to be bothered, so I left. I found myself unable to function and unable to find work. I wandered in the City streets for a while, then the Human Resources people took me to this Homeless Shelter in Harlem. I am merely surviving, eating at the soup kitchens and panhandling in the subway."

"I am at the Veterans Shelter on 2nd Ave. Would you want to move there so we can be together? Joseph pondered for one moment. "Sgt., are you comfortable there? What amenities do they offer?" "They are accepting veterans only, of course. It is not as crowded as the ordinary shelter. They also offer meals on Sundays at a very low price, although you have the option to eat anywhere you like. More important to

me is, they treat you with more respect." Sound good!

My place of residence is not one you could be proud of.

Take me to your abode." Danilo slapped his buddy's

palm. "Good! Then we can be buddies again!"

Sitting under the stairway of the No. 2,3 and 4

train station after Joseph had registered at the Veterans'

Shelter, the two friends continued their chat. "I have

a job prospect in Montauk, Long Island, a janitor

position in a new Children's School. They won't need

me until the opening in June this year." You are lucky,

pal. I don't have any prospect. They had posted a few

job openings at my shelter, but they were for skilled

workers. You know I don't have any skill." I guess I will have to continue begging until I get myself a job, any job at all."

"Keep looking and keep hoping, my friend." They became silent when a well-dressed woman passed by and deposited a dollar bill into Joseph's hat. They remained in their spot in the subway until late in the afternoon. They had collected only six dollars between the two of them.

As they were getting out of the train station entrance, they heard a loud crash. Boom! Instinctively, they ran out into the street to see what was happening. A dump truck plowed into a black Mercedes Benz right outside the station entrance. The two buddies

rushed to the scene. They saw a boy strapped to his

seat, injured badly and was crying. The woman beside

him appeared unconscious. The driver was slumped

on the steering wheel.

Danilo pried open the car door, while Joseph

ran after the driver of the truck who was trying to

escape the accident scene. "Please, somebody call the

ambulance!" Danilo took the car seat with the boy

in it and deposited it gently on the sidewalk. He held

the boy's hand and comforted him. While Danlo was

waiting for the ambulance, Joseph came back with

the truck driver in tow. "Hold him for the police." He

asked a man bystander.

"Boom! Another explosion! The Mercedes car

was engulfed with fire from its engine. People were

screaming and running away. There was no time to get

the two unconscious people from inside the burning

vehicle. An ambulance arrived shortly and took the

injured boy. The two men insisted to go with the boy

in the ambulance. The firemen arrived at the scene

as the ambulance was speeding towards the nearest

hospital.

They were hanging out at the hospital

lobby outside the emergency room when a

distinguished-looking couple approached them.

They felt little and humble with their ragged clothes

in front of the obviously well-off people. The lady

spoke first. "The emergency crew told us that you

two had rescued our boy. We are very grateful." The

man came closer and shook Danilo's hand, then

Joseph's.

"We only did what anyone would have done

under the circumstances, sir, madam." Danilo said

humbly, standing up from the couch. "Yes, but your

instant action save our son's life. That was heroic of you

both. We do not know how to express our gratitude,"

the man said, obviously the husband, without releasing

Danilo's hand. "That was nothing compared with what we had done in Vietnam," Joseph remarked, standing up beside Danilo. "I am Danilo and my buddy here is Joseph." Danilo did the introductions.

"Oh! So you are Vietnam veterans then?" The couple became more curious. My husband, Jeffrey here, was an admiral in the Navy, serving during the later part of the war." The woman put her arms around her husband. Joseph and Danilo executed salutes, which the admiral returned. "Now, my fellow soldiers, how about dinner with us? Our meeting is a cause for celebration." The couple stepped aside and conferred.

"My husband says we should all go to Astoria Manor Restaurant in Astoria, but I say, let's have dinner at our house in Forest Hills, near Kew Gardens. By the way, please call me Consuelo. Which is your choice, brave soldiers?" "We will leave it to you, sir Jeffrey and madam Consuelo." The couple went back to the emergency room to check on their son. While they waited, Joseph remarked. "Sergeant, I am a bit ashamed to go with them. We are not dressed decently." Before Danilo could say anything, the couple came back looking happy.

The group piled into a sleek, red Jaguar. While

they were on Queens Blvd., Queens, Consuelo said

enthusiastically. "Our son, Christopher is doing well.

He should be out from Queens General Hospital

tomorrow and moved to Presbyterian Hospital in the

city for a more thorough check up and rehabilitation.

His doctor said that no complications are expected and

he should be up and running soon. That is another cause for celebration."

In Forest Hills, they entered a spacious lawn bordered with maples and pines. The grounds was handsomely kept with flowers scattered around the area. Consuelo spoke with one of the housemaids who came back later with two sets of clothing for Danilo and Joseph. "They are part of Christopher's uncle's wardrobe. Don't worry if they don't fit you well. We shall have you both fitted by our tailor tomorrow." Danilo and Joseph were too overwhelmed to say anything.

During dinner, Admiral Jeffrey told the two soldiers that the woman with Christopher in the accident was his governess. They were on their way to a Birthday Party in a family friend's home on Madison Avenue. She had been with the family since their first child out of four was a baby, eleven years ago. She would be terribly missed. He quickly changed the sad episode and turned to the men. "What do you do now, our great nation's heroes?" Neither could speak for a moment. Then Joseph boldly said, "We have no work at present, sir, and are merely trying to survive."

"We are managing, sir." Danilo said briefly.

Two weeks afterwards, an express mail for Danilo and Joseph was delivered at the shelter. It was from Admiral and Mrs. Jeffrey Hamilton. It read: "Our boy is back home, thanks to you both! Two separate letters came with the note, recommendations for an Assistant Manager in their farm in Rosedale, Long Island, and for a manager position in their other farm in Great Neck, Long Island. "Let us know if you like to take up the positions we are offering you." The note concluded.

Danilo and Joseph confirmed their acceptance of the job offers. They were the most important guests at Christopher's fifth birthday party that summer.

# CHAPTER 12

## Treasure in the Dump

O n the sixth night in Tampa babysitting for her grandchildren, grandma was busy packing up her clothes for the trip back home the next day. A loud knocking interrupted her.

Small feet came inside. "Grandma, you said the other night that you still have another story to tell?"

"Surely, but children, your mom might want to spend time with you. She is arriving tomorrow afternoon from California. She must have missed you so much."

"Mommy is coming home!" The two kids jumped with joy. Tell us another story tonight, grandma." Olivia begged.

"Yes, sweetie pie. In fact, I have two more stories after tonight's story that I have not yet told you. She led the children to the family room where they could all sit comfortably. Angela called by long distance before they could settle down on the family room couch. She had to stay for another day in L.A. The conference had ended but they were requested to remain for one more day for the coming of the

Governor. A banquet had been arranged on their last night.

My last story is about two homeless men. One was Arnold, 37 years old widower, who lost his job as a construction worker after an accident that resulted in the loss of one of his arms. The other man was Jesse, 32 years old who had never been married. He had been out of job for almost a year. He was laid off by an auto spare parts company where he had worked for 8 years along with half of his co-workers due to the company's financial problems. They shared a shanty near a garbage dump area in the outskirts of the city. They could be seen often at the soup kitchens eating their meals on Sundays and at the railroad station panhandling. They preferred begging at the railway station than in the subway because they wanted to avoid the police. Besides, they did not have as much competition at the railroad station as in the subway.

Once, the beggars in the subways were herded by the city police and dumped in the Homeless Shelter. The two buddies could not stand the chaos, the crowded common room accommodation, the fighting of gang residents and the filth. They moved to the dump area which was not only quiet but they were mostly alone, except during occasional days when other scavengers came picking garbage.

Their shanty was well hidden by three large garbage trucks that were abandoned because they were too old to be of service. During winter time, they would go back to the shelter to seek refuge from the extreme cold. One winter, they did not want to leave their shanty. Arnold caught pneumonia and almost died. Jesse brought him to the City Public Hospital where he remained for two weeks. Jesse himself almost got sick too. Since then, they either stayed in the shelter or in the subway washroom during the winter months.

Every night, Arnold and Jesse stayed up very late inside their shanty, listening to their portable radio.

It was their only source of entertainment. Arnold had a favorite movie series that lasted for one hour and Jesse's favorite was the sports reports. There was no conflict since they obliged each other's preferences. One particular day, they overslept until the middle of the morning.

A loud rumble and a heavy crash woke the two men from their slumber. They opened their eyes to the piles and piles of garbage raining on them. There was no time to escape. Their shanty made of cardboard boxes was buried under the truckload of garbage. They were trapped! Worst, the frail shanty gave way to the weight of the garbage. Neither could move.

Jesse's two feet were pinned down by a large, heavy wood plank. Arnold was choking from the smelly filth that covered his head and body.

Arnold eventually freed himself of his prison of garbage after minutes of struggle. He pushed and he clawed at the assorted types of garbage until only bits of food refuse covered his aching body. Jesse could not move his legs. The wood plank was heavier than he had thought. He struggled to wriggle himself from his shackles, but he was too weak from the blow on his shoulder. Obviously, the plank struck his shoulder then fell on his legs.

They lay helpless for a awhile. Arnold finally regained some strength. At least, he was not pinned down like his buddy. He poked slowly around until he could see some sunlight that filtered through the mound of garbage. "Jesse, hang on, boy! I shall help you out of your shackle shortly." He made a tunnel through the heap of all sorts of garbage, rotting food, bulbs, kitchen tools, broken plates, batteries, old flashlights and many other types of discarded materials.

After what seemed forever, he finally made it to the end of his tunnel, revealing a bright noonday sun. Happily, he went back to his friend who continued to try to get off his bondage. "Oh! Ha! Ha!" Jesse was howling in spite of his helpless situation. "What's the matter with you, pal? Have you gone mad?" "Ho! Ho! Ha!" Jesse continued his mirth. "No, sir, I'm far from mad! I've got a kick looking at you. Oh, man, you look so hilarious!"

There was no mirror. Arnold started to touch his face, his head, shoulders and the rest of his body. He did not notice it before but he could now smell himself. He could now imagine how he looked. No wonder his friend had a ball looking at him. He broke into a loud laughter. The two otherwise miserable men joined each other in prolonged, hysterical laughter.

Arnold struggled to move the plank of wood from his friend's leg. It took some time, but laughing while doing something though how hard it was, helped a lot.

Arnold and Jesse surveyed their immediate surroundings when they finally got out of their smelly and rough accommodation. The area was like a forest of garbage. Obviously, the garbage men did early dumping and covered the areas that were not used before. There were boxes of old cereal, overripe fruits, old half pint milk, which were probably expired, empty cartons and cans, household things, old clothing, and many other assortment of stuff.

The two men salvaged all the foodstuff they could find, loaded them into a large box and headed to where their hut once stood. "We have to build another hut, Jess. I don't feel like going into the subway for shelter." Yes, let's do that, but first I say let's eat." While they ate, Arnold remarked between bites of an overripe banana. "Know what? I am about to quit, Buddy. I am sick of this life we have chosen to lead." "What do you intend to do? Rob a bank?" Jesse asked, putting down an empty carton of milk.

"Of course, not. I could never be a robber, or anything that is against the law. I could be a beggar forever, if I have to. What about you? Do you have anything in mind?" None whatsoever. I think I would prefer to be living this kind of life, free and without cares, instead of being shackled with a life that keeps me from doing what I want to do." Freedom is one thing," Arnold pointed out, "not knowing where to go for our next meal or where to sleep is another." "Let's get on with looking for materials for a new home." He changed the subject. They headed to the new mound of garbage that were hauled only that morning.

Jess, look at what I just found!" Arnold was lifting a cloth bag. It was so heavy that he staggered while holding it up. "Did you hear me? Look!" He put down the bag and started to untie the rope around it.

What he saw inside almost made him pass out. Coins!

One dollar coins! Jesse did not hear him because he

just found a bag too. It looked like the other bag that

Arnold just found. "My God! What is this?" Jesse

gasped in utter amazement as he opened the bag full

of dollar bills. Putting down the items close to each

other, the two buddies danced around the piles of

garbage, singing and chanting incoherent words.

What to do with their precious findings occupied

the two men's minds. "I think we should turn these

monies to the police. Someone might be searching for

them." Arnold finally said. "Why should we do that?

These monies were thrown away, maybe by someone

who took pity on us. Do you believe in miracles?"

Jesse, the always practical one said with conviction.

They argued for a while.

"Let's draw lots. This way, no one is subject to blame if this fortune we just found is indeed someone's lost property." Arnold declared. He took a dollar coin and tossed it. He lost. Jesse jumped with delight. "My friend, good luck is on us. I firmly believe that this money is really intended for us." They decided not to do anything with the money for a while. They buried the bags in one corner of the garbage lot then went into town to buy a newspaper in case the lost money was mentioned. They read the paper and listened to the radio news for a few days but there was no report

about the money. Arnold and Jess left their town and

settled in a far state. They both remarried. The two

close buddies lived happier, comfortable lives with

their families ever after.

Grandma did not tell the children about their

mommy's extended stay in L.A. She hoped they would

forget about her supposed arrival in the afternoon of the following day. After they had done their homework, grandma told them. "Children, how about a swim in the residents' swimming pool before dinner time? I'll pack our dinner and we can have a picnic there." The two kids hugged her tightly with joy. This was the second time they would be swimming in the pool. They did not eat at the pool then. They had their dinner at the Boston Market restaurant with Jasmine's children. This picnic would be new to them.

After she had packed the Salisbury steak, Brian's favorite, Chicken Adobo, Olivia's favorite, baked potatoes with boiled string beans on the side, fruits and water, grandma checked the kids' swimming suits.

Brian's swimming trunk was a bit tight. She went

back upstairs to get a replacement. The swimming

pool was a walking distance away, so they did not

take the car. They did not get back home until late in

the afternoon. Grandma put on the television set for

their favorite cartoons while they rested on the couch.

# CHAPTER 13

## Jojo and Theo

"My story tonight is a short one," grandma said to her grandchildren after they had watched the cartoons. She saw that Brian was yawning but Olivia appeared anxious to hear her story. Grandma sat in the middle of the two kids, as she always did during her storytelling. "Grandma, I want popcorn, the sweet one." Brian suddenly sat up from lying on grandma's lap. "I'll make it!" Olivia volunteered. "Be careful, sweetheart. Wait a little while before opening the hot bag."

Jojo was a three year old brown and black pony and Theo was an active five year old gray Terrier. Jojo was the pet of the youngest, six year old son, Aaron. Theo was Joshua's, Aaron's older brother's pet. Aaron considered the dog as his second pet. Joshua took pleasure having the dog chase his horse wherever he was heading to. He was an expert young horse rider. He won in a horse race last fall. The family was horse breeders in their spacious ten acre farm. Theo was one of the Cruz' family's eight dogs. Aaron would take Theo with him when he was riding across the fields outside the farm after school hours most days.

He would go on riding until he got tired. Theo would

be panting heavily and too exhausted after each long

chase.

One day, Theo was chasing Joshua's horse when

he fell into a newly dug well. Joshua's helpers got him

out after hours of work. When they finally got the

poor dog out, it lost half of its fore legs. They took

him to a veterinarian and was rehabilitated, but Theo

was never the same again after the accident. He could

no longer chase his master's horse. Joshua no longer

gave the attention he usually would give to Theo.

Once or twice, he would kick the poor dog when

Theo attempted to follow him around the house, limping. He would not even pet him anymore. Joshua got himself a new pet, a black German Shepherd. Theo felt not only sad but jealous of his master's new dog. Theo nuzzled his nose on Joshua's neck while the man was napping in the veranda one afternoon. How he had missed his buddy! Joshua got so mad that he grabbed Theo by the neck, dragged him out into the yard and instructed a groomsman to throw the dog into the train tracks. Theo kept on coming back to the farm, if only to have a glimpse of his previous master.

On the other hand, Jojo, the pony was not at all living an easy life. His young master, Aaron, would regularly ride him across their spacious lawn back and forth under the heat of the sun, beating him up when the poor pony showed slowing down. Once, the pony refused to go on any further after a couple of hours running around the lawn carrying his young master. Aaron dismounted and beat Jojo up with a stick. This was a regular routine and after he himself would get tired, Aaron would just leave Jojo under the sun until the groomsman had the time to put him back inside the barn, usually hours afterwards.

Theo watched Jojo's ordeal with sympathy. He could no longer bear his own master's maltreatment of him. Seeing Jojo in a similar situation, he decided to do something. One dark night, he went into the barn and spoke to Jojo. The poor pony was lying on the dried hay, breathing heavily from the day's ordeal. "My friend, would you like to join me on a trip?" Trip? Where to?" Anywhere, everywhere, away from this dismal place and cruel people." How do you propose to begin this trip? When do we start? "Right now. Just follow me." Theo said to Jojo with the confidence of someone who knew exactly what he was going to do.

They walked and walked in the dark, Theo in the lead and Jojo close on his heels. It was dawn when they came to a river. Jojo and Theo hesitated. "What do we do now? This river is deep. I know because once, my master attempted to cross it and was not able to because the current is also strong," Jojo said as they rested on the river's bank. Theo sat with his friend as they watched the swift, passing current. "Let's rest for a while. Later, let's find some food and move on downstream to find a shallower part of the river."

The two animals were fast asleep when a boat carrying three passengers anchored nearby. "Hi! Look! Can you believe this? Beautiful animals!" A young boy and a woman wearing a scarf approached the two sleeping animals. The third man was left behind tying up the boat to a tree trunk.

"Alfonso, we have found treasures!" The woman

delightedly exclaimed. Theo and Jojo awoke from their

deep sleep by the petting of the three strangers. They

both got up and stared at the two middle age people

and the boy, maybe 10 years old. Theo edged closer

to his friend protectively, although he instinctively

knew that they did not only look harmless but kind

and sympathetic.

The woman stooped and petted Theo again.

"Where did you come from? Would you like to be

my pet? I so long for a dog like you." "And mama,

I would like to have this pony. I will look after

him well and take him for a ride. I shall have aunt

Helena make a nice saddle made of cloth for him."

"Now, wait a minute, what about the owners of these animals?" The man, obviously the husband, was doubtful. "Don't worry. Let's put up their pictures in the papers and see if their owners would claim them. The wife said confidently.

The family hired a cart to take Theo and Jojo to their home upriver. No one put a claim on the two animals, so they lived happily in the loving care of the Benson family, who were prominent residents of a gated community far from where the animals came from.

"Grandma, can I have a pony?" Brian was no longer drowsy. "And grandma, I would like to have a pet dog," said Olivia. Let's wait for mom and see what she says." Let us sleep now."

"Grandma, when is our mom coming home?" Brian asked before he slipped under the covers. "Mom said she is arriving at five in the afternoon tomorrow. "We are going to meet her at the airport." Yes! Yes! Yes! "The children said happily at the same time. Would you want a glass of milk before going to bed, Brian?" The boy nodded. "I also want it, grandma." Olivia got up and followed her grandma to the kitchen downstairs. "What's your story tonight, grandma?"

"We are going to sleep early tonight, so my story is a short one, shorter than last night's. It is a story about a woman who dreamed about heaven."

## A Glimpse of Heaven?

It was past midnight. The house near the lake was quiet. Not even the soft howling of the wind or the chirping of cicadas could be heard. Nena tiptoed from her children's bedrooms after checking on them. Nanette, 14 and Lorna, 10 who were sharing the same room were fast asleep. Arthur, 16, slept in the adjacent room. Nena's aunt, Josefa, 82 years old occupied the guest room on the first floor of the house.

Josefa just had a major operation and did not have anyone to look after her in Arizona where she lived alone in a Senior Development Community. She was the lone survivor in her family of eight, consisting of her parents and five sisters. Nena and her family took her in until she was well enough to go home. During the past two days, Josefa had not been too well. Nena would take her to her physician-surgeon for a follow-up checkup the following day. She appeared to be asleep when Nena checked on her tonight.

Leo, Nena's husband was snoring and did not stir when his wife joined him in bed. Nena had stayed up late watching her favorite movie series. As she was preparing for bed and dimming her bedside lamp, she heard a loud scream from the guest room."No No! Let me stay! Please let me stay!" Nena ran downstairs thinking that an intruder might have entered the house. When she entered the guest room, she saw her aunt sitting up in bed, wide awake.

"Weren't you just screaming? What happened?" Nena asked anxiously. Josefa took a deep breath and said, "I just had a dream, a beautiful, happy dream. It was so vivid that I thought it was real. I wish it were real!" She sighed again. I would like to tell you about it now while it is still fresh in my mind. What time is it?" "Half past 1:00 a.m. Go back to sleep, auntie. You can tell your story during breakfast tomorrow."

The next morning was a Saturday so the children were at home. Leo, a bank consultant did not work on Saturdays. His wife, Nena was a full time homemaker. They chatted merrily about the forthcoming fair during the next weekend, when Nena remembered her cousin's dream experience. "Guys, guys! Aunt Josefa had an interesting dream last night that she wants to share with us. She turned to her aunt who was seated beside her at the table.

"I was going through a very well lighted tunnel that did not seem to have an end. After walking for some time, I finally came out into a straight, narrow path. The end of the path was obscured by white clouds. I kept on walking until I arrived at the entrance to a beautiful, brightly lighted, arched gate. Two robed men were at the entrance on either side of the gate. There were at least five people ahead of me on the line. One was denied entrance for some reason. The four people disappeared from sight after they were ushered inside."

"When it was my turn, the older man with a beard looked me up from head to foot. Then he spoke to the younger man in a language I did not understand.

Finally, the older man said to me. "You are not due here yet. But because your folks are anxious to see you, you will be allowed to come in. However, you cannot remain here for more than an hour. You have to get back home until you are ready to settle here." He signaled for me to proceed."

I walked on ahead, not certain where I was heading to. The road had become very wide and smooth like it was paved with shiny granite. Along the road there were hundreds of flowers and grasses that looked immaculately maintained. The air was fragrant with the smell of assorted flowers. I could not see the sky overhead, only the sun shining brightly overhead as if it was suspended in the air. There was faint, sweet music from many instruments.

When I turned a bend, I saw a group of people waving at me from under a cluster of beautiful trees grouped together. As I drew near, I recognized each one of them. I exclaimed happily. "Mama! Papa! My dear sisters!" I tried to embrace my mama first, but I could not feel her body. I only heard her say, "My dear child. It is so good to see you. We had been anxious to have you here with us." My father leaned forward and held my two hands. I could not feel his hand clasping mine! My other sisters looked on smiling.

"Where is Remy, our oldest?" I just noticed that my family was not complete. None of them answered me in a while. Then, mama took me aside and said in a sad voice. "Your oldest sister is in a temporary place. We were told by the master that she is on probation." I was going to ask what she had done, and who the master was, but my sisters motioned to me to follow them. We all walked together towards a big house all lit up with incandescent lamps from the posts to the roof tops. The sight was blinding.

Inside the wonder house, my mother seated me beside her. My father sat at the other end of the big table. We were served our meal of numerous dishes by white clothed waiters on silver trays that gleamed as they moved around serving. My mother said to me in a tender, loving voice. "My dearest youngest daughter, now that we are together, we shall never part again." She offered me her favorite dishes, the dishes she used to cook for our dinners before. "Eat more, my child. You look so thin. You have not been taking care of yourself."

After the meal, my older sister played the harp and my father played the saxophone. The rest of my sisters sang. My mother put on the phonograph that she inherited from her parents. Soon, the house was filled with unearthly music. I felt overwhelmed with happiness. I danced with pure joy, twirling and swaying like I used to do during our family get togethers when I was a child. Everybody was enjoying themselves, clapping and stamping our feet.

Our fun was interrupted by the arrival of two young white robed men. They spoke to my father and mother. My mother looked at me with teary eyes while my father appeared to be begging the men for something. Finally, he came up to me and said sadly. "My little one, they are taking you now. You were given only an hour to spend with us." My mother and my sisters hugged me one by one. "Goodbye, darling." They all wept. Even my father whom I had never seen crying before was tearful. The two men each held my hand and prodded me to go with them. I refused to leave. I screamed and screamed! Then I awoke from the dream."

"That was when I heard you screaming." Going around to her aunt, and wiping away the tears from her aunt's eyes, Nena said. "What an unbelievable dream, auntie!" The whole family was silent for a while, then Lorna, the youngest daughter came closer to her grand aunt and said. "Don't worry, grand auntie. You will go back there again and be with them one day." Strangely, Josefa got well completely and lived to be ninety years old.

At the end of the story on the last night with her young grandchildren, Brian sat up from bed and said seriously. "Grandma, I should like to go to that beautiful place."Olivia also sat up from her side of the bed and rebuked her little brother.

"How would you go there, my little, dumb brother? That story that grandma told us was only a dream. She turned to her grandma. "Is there really a place like it, grandma? Is there a name for it?" Grandma hesitated. How would she answer the question honestly? She herself does not even know if there was such a place. Maybe Heaven? She hugged her grandchildren back and said with all honesty and conviction. "My sweet grandchildren. Yes, there is a place like the one in my dream story. However, no one has yet gone there and came back to tell his/her story. The name of the wonderful place is heaven. What we can do is to continue to believe that there is such a place and try hard to be as good as we can be because only the good people go there."

"But I am a good boy, grandma, am I not?"

"Indeed, you are, my boy. Continue to be so. Let us now say our evening prayers, "Angel of God" and hope that we shall dream a beautiful dream such as the one I just told you tonight."

Olivia and Brian

# Grandma Lydia Says "Goodbye"

In the afternoon of the following day, Angela

was coming out from the Luggage Claim area, United

Airlines, when her mother in-law, her two children,

Olivia and Brian rushed forward to welcome her.

The two children hugged their mother for the

longest time. Grandma gave her daughter in-law a kiss on the check. "Welcome back, Angela! Did you have a nice trip?" "Yes, mostly. There was only a brief turbulence halfway here." She kissed her two children again and asked them to sit at the bench while she retrieved her luggage.

After her final packing for her train trip back to Chicago, she went to the family room where Angela and the kids were watching a new movie, which she brought back from Los Angeles, California, "Marty and Me," a dog movie." Grandma watched the movie with them until halfway through. Their mother wanted to retire early since she had stayed up very late the other night.

"Say goodnight and goodbye to your grandma now, children. She will be leaving at noontime tomorrow. You will be in school so you won't be able to see her off." Olivia hugged grandma first. "Grandma, I wish you would stay longer with us." The girl wiped away her tears. Brian came closer and kissed her on the check. "When will you come back here, grandma? Soon, o.k.?" His voice was small and sad.

Grandma tried hard to keep her tears in check. "I shall not be back until months from now. But don't worry. You and your mom will be coming to

Chicago in June, three months from today. Right, dear? Angela nodded. We shall see each other again soon, my darlings." She hugged both children tightly and followed them upstairs to the bedrooms. Before Angela had tucked them in their beds, grandma kissed the children once again and said. "God bless you both and your mom always." She waited until the children had said their night prayers before she headed to her bedroom on the other side of the floor, feeling sad that she had to leave the following day.

# PART II

## Senior Stories

Gabriella, Stephanie, Alexandra

A month after grandma came back from Tampa,

she got a phone call from Stephanie.

The girl sounded enthusiastic. "Grandma, we shall be coming to Huntley on your birthday in June, all three of us, Gabriella, Alexandra and myself. Our daddy had already sent us our tickets. Isn't it wonderful?" She blabbered on the phone happily.

Grandma was speechless on the other end of the line. Then she heard Alexandra on another phone. "Our auntie Bing, Uncle Ariel and our daddy are hosting a big party for you. We can't almost wait to come!"

"That's awfully nice! I am totally surprised!" Grandma Lydia finally spoke. Then she heard Mari, their mom's voice. "Lydia, this was supposed to be a secret. Bing and Ariel did not want you to know about it. It was supposed to be a surprise." Oh, but I

am surprised already!" She heard the three laughing.

"Grandma, please don't tell Auntie Bing that you

already know about it,' Stephanie spoke again. "No, I

won't. I will just pretend that I heard nothing of your

little secret." Grandma smiled in spite of herself.

The three girls arrived three days before their

grandma's birthday. They were to stay for only two

weeks because they had a lot lined up throughout

the summer. They planned to stay with grandma at

Del Webb for four days, and the rest of the days with

their aunt and uncle. Bing, her daughter had a lot of

interesting places to spend with the girls, including

at the Wisconsin Dells, the Holy Hills in Wisconsin, Lake Geneva and many other spots in the city. They were still very young when they visited the city of Chicago and wanted to see them again and cover more places, especially Gabriella who was only a baby when she came to Chicago ten years ago.

The birthday party for grandma, who turned 75, was attended by all her daughter and son in-law's friends. Her son Clyde arrived from Detroit the day before. Dante, her nephew living in Toronto, Canada also came with his three children and wife. Gabriella did a Judo/Karate exhibition, Stephanie sang and Alexandra danced during the impromptu program.

It had been the best birthday party grandma ever had in many years. Gifts almost filled the back of her car.

Grandma spent the afternoons in the patio with her grandchildren, eating ice cream or drinking homemade smoothies. Mornings saw them at the Stingray Bay pool or at Del Webb's outdoor pool, or at the mall. These were the things they did every summer when they were still younger. During one afternoon on the girls' second day, while they were at the front veranda eating grandma's hot siopao, (steamed rolls with chicken filling) Stephanie called out to her grandma who was in the kitchen.

"Grandma, you used to tell us bedtime stories when we came here a few summers ago. I can still remember those adventures vividly when you were young, growing in your farm." "I do too. I love those stories about the butterflies, the bees about the leeches, about the numerous fruits in your farm and others." Alexandra was quick to reinforce her sister's comments.

"My cousins had told me about some of your stories when I was not able to come with them. Would you like to tell some of them again now grandma?" Gabriella asked, taking the pitcher of lemonade from her grandmother. "I'd love to, Gabriella, but perhaps you are now too old to hear childhood stories. Anyway, I have written those stories in my first memoir. Let me see what I can tell you today while we are having our snacks."

"What about if you tell us about your experiences when you were working in New York after you returned from Nigeria?" Stephanie suggested. "Yeah, yeah, that would be better than repeating the stories you have already told us, grandma dear." Alexandra declared. "Let me see. Yes, I have told you girls, stories about my life from when I was very young to when I grew up, got married and worked in Nigeria. I have interesting experiences with seniors while I worked as Case Manager and Entitlement

Specialist in Queens, New York from 1989 to when

I retired in 2007 after Joe died.

I was first employed at a State-funded program,

called Early Childhood Foundation as Case manager,

helping young mothers and their children. I held

babysitting classes and conducted a group called,

"Mommy and me," in addition to advocating for them

and helping them with benefits applications. I held

the position for one year and was transferred to a

program funded by the city and the state, managed

by Catholic Charities. My group of four started the

Food and Nutrition Program or (F.A.N) Program in

Jamaica, Queens. We provided once a month supply of basic foodstuffs to our clients consisting of low-income families with young children from infant to six years old, the cut off age, and to pregnant women.

After a year and a half, my supervisor recommended me for a vacant position as Case manager, Entitlement Specialist and Food and Nutrition Lecturer at a senior center in Long Island City, New York. Barely a year afterwards, I was promoted to handle four senior centers in Southwest, Queens, providing the same services to seniors sixty and above. The combined total of my clients was 260 from all four centers in Woodhaven, St. Mary's,

Richmond Hill and Ozone Park, Queens, funded

by the Department for the Aging and sponsored by

Catholic Charities.

"Did you go to all four centers everyday,

grandma?" A thoughtful question from Stephanie.

"No, dear. I alternated between them during the week,

two days in each center. "Did you ride in the subway,

or took the bus to go to work, grandma?" Gabriella

asked. "Oh no. I drove to and from work in a new car,

a Chevy Z- 24, a gift from Joe when we were newly

married. Before I received my New York License, I

took the subway for some time and Joe would meet me

at the train station closer to home. I could not use my

old Driving License, of course, and the job of getting

a New York License was rather tough."

My job was a multi-task one. I helped the needy

seniors apply for benefits and entitlements such as

Food Stamps, Medicaid, SSI and Public Assistance,

Public Housing, did crisis intervention, Referrals,

counseling and advocacy, visited the sick seniors at

hospitals and at home, went to court to testify for

clients who were victims of elderly abuse and for other

cases and attended funerals."How were you able to do

all your duties, grandma? They seem pretty hard to

do." Alexandra put in after being quiet for some time.

"My profession is related to social work. I was well experienced in dealing with people, situations and issues when I was a teacher in the Philippines and in Nigeria. I also attended a lot of job orientation, workshops Seminars and conferences for professional advancement. I found my job very satisfying, fulfilling and rewarding. I realized that one does not have to attend Social Work School to do social work. If you for instance help and reach out to others in need in any way you could, empathize with them, offer genuine sympathy in their grief and be a true friend without expecting any return from them, you are doing social work.

"What kind of people did you work with, grandma?" Stephanie asked. This time, grandma felt being interrogated by her grandchildren, but she was only too happy to answer their inquiries. Asking the kind of questions they asked her was a sign of interest and intelligence. "My clients were of different ethnic backgrounds and races. There were Italians, Spanish, Canadians, Irish and English, Polish and Lithuanians and from other parts of Europe who either migrated here when they were young or were born here of foreign parents. "I had client members at the centers who came from Asia, the Philippines, China, Japan, Indonesia, from the Caribbean nations and a couple of seniors from as far as Australia. Most of my clients were Hispanics, from Mexico, Honduras, Uruguay, Venezuela, Ecuador, Colombia, Puerto Rico, Panama, etc. As a result of my dealings with mostly Spanish-speaking seniors, my ability to speak Spanish was very much enhanced.

"How old were your clients, grandma?" Gabriella asked. "Oh, I think earlier on, I mentioned that our senior members at the centers were from sixty above, meaning there were sixty year olds, whom we called young seniors, to 105 years old. The majority were in their seventies and eighties, a few in their nineties and two over 100 years old."

"I enjoyed working with seniors during my eighteen years working with them. There were so many challenges and I rose to them with determination and with expertise, which improved through years of dedicated service. Each client who came to me for help was needy, not only financially but in adequate housing, food, clothing, social and psychological needs. Some few were self-sufficient and needed only an ear to listen to them about their physical woes. Many were living alone and needed a place to socialize and congregate. The senior center was a perfect, welcome place for them."

"So, grandma, what other things did they do at the senior centers? Did they only come to see you for help?" Stephanie asked another of her thoughtful questions. "Our centers offered a lot more than that. We had congregate hot lunch every day, which the seniors paid for only at minimal cost because they were subsidized by the agency. The meals were delivered to each center by refrigerated vans from the main center that prepared the hot meals. We also had Meals On Wheels Program for homebound senior members, the handicapped and the sick who could not come to the center."

We had once a month birthday parties for each of the center celebrants of the month, with live music from a paid musician. Special lunches were served during these occasions. We had also once a month trips to the casinos in Atlantic City, New Jersey once a month, card games, blood pressure screenings, dancing, exercise and singing activities, health lectures from health professionals, and other lectures other than Food and Nutrition Citizenship and English as a Second language lectures which I handled. Our centers would house seniors who had no air conditioner during the very hot months and stay in during winter when they did not have heat at home. We also offered rides to and from the center for only twenty five cents per trip.

"Wow! Grandma. Your senior centers in New York sound great. Do we have such centers here in Illinois?" Alexandra asked, very pleased. Before her grandma could reply, Gabriella put in her remarks. "Sounds to me like the senior centers in New York during your time there was like a second home to the senior population." "Exactly. That was why and how the centers were put up in the first place. To answer Alexandra's question, yes, but I think there are quite a few in this state, and if there are, they probably offer limited services. They must have them also in Florida. I will look them up in the internet."

"How were the centers run? By you, grandma or by someone else?" Stephanie inquired intelligently. We had Site managers that managed each center, an assistant if available, a cleaning staff and some volunteers. The centers were run mostly by volunteers. The main center, Ozone Park Senior Center located in the center of southwest Queens, the biggest among the four centers had more paid staff because they prepared the meals everyday at that site for senior center lunches and for homebound meals.

I would sometimes assume the duties of the Site Manager when the person took leave of absence. When this situation would occur, I would be saddled with more things to do, my own duties as well as managing the center activities as well. We had supervisors from the Department for the Aging, our funding source, and from Catholic Charities, Archdiocese of Brooklyn and Queens. Once a year we had a thorough evaluation of each center, including meal service, activities provided, senior attendance and staff performance.

"Grandma, did you have any vacation days?" Alexandra asked. "I had 21 days total paid leave days in a year and I would spend my vacation days traveling.

Also I had a week sick leave a year."Your work seem very interesting, but I think it was rather hectic, don't you think, Alexandra, Gabriella?" "Indeed, Stephanie. My duties were varied, duties in fact that social workers did, even more. It was a pity that they could not give me the title of "Social Worker" in my job description because I did not have a social work degree. But I enjoyed my job and worked hard until I retired when Joe died. I loved working with the seniors and I think they loved me too. They were very sad when I retired. Many did not go to the centers any more after I left." I was very sad too. The seniors became like family to me, dear to my heart.

I realized that when you gained their trust, they would get out of their shells and pour out to you everything about their lives. You could not help but give yourself wholeheartedly too, like a son or daughter to their parents. I regretted my leaving them. Some wrote and called me and told me that two of the centers were closed due to lack of participation and lack of funding. That was a pity.

It was late in the afternoon when grandma rose from her lounging chair in the patio. The three girls remained seated, finishing their lemonade drink. Stephanie held grandma's hand and said. "Grandma, we thought you were a great social worker. Are you not going to tell us stories about the seniors whom you had helped?" "Oh yes. I got carried away. I had helped so many during my eighteen years working with them. I will only tell stories about five or six of them. Now, we have to postpone the story telling until during dinner or after dinner. Let me see how my pot roast is doing."

"We are waiting for your stories, grandma, dear." Alexandra said in between bites of the pot roast. "Alright, but first, how is my pot roast? "Oh, um! Super, grandma." The girls exclaimed simultaneously. "Teach me how to make it, yes, grandma? "Yes dear, before you girls leave two days from now. By the way, Gabriella won in a cooking contest last month, did you know? How much was your prize, dear?" "$400.00 dollars." "Wow! May I borrow some, my dear, talented cousin?" Alexandra asked smiling. "I went on a shopping spree with my mom. Whatever I have left, I'll treat you both to ice cream and drinks during our outing with Auntie Bing."

"Now, I think I am ready to tell my stories. Are you ready to listen, girls?" She got everyone's attention. The events in my stories truly happened but the names of the seniors involved have been altered to protect their identities. I think most or all the seniors

I used to help are now dead, or if they are still alive,

they would be in their nineties, or 100's. Bless them!"

# Rosa

I first met Rosa on my second day at St. Mary's

Senior Center in Long Island City, New York. She was

a vivacious, petite old 79 year old lady and a widow.

Her two sons lived in another state. She was fond of

wearing make up, sometimes so heavy that she looked

like a doll. Her friends used to make fun of her. They

told me secretly that Rosa had a boyfriend. She lived

alone in an old, rent-controlled apartment only five

minutes ride by bus to the center. She often walked to and from the center.

Rosa never missed going to the center. She was the secretary to the Senior Club and did her recording of minutes of the meetings with much enthusiasm. She was always willing to help decorating the center during holidays. During lunch times, she would help distribute the food trays to the seniors on the line and helped put away the used trays after the meal. She would eat only when everyone had been served. She was a sweet, caring old lady. Sometimes I thought that she would have made a good social worker. But she did not even have high school education.

During the birthday party for the birthday celebrants of the month, Rosa would dance to her heart's content to the live music provided by Angelo Muto, the musician for all four centers, paid for by center funds. Rosa loved Angelo. She would serve him lunch personally and reserved his snacks after the dance. The other seniors accused her of flirting with Angelo. I would dismiss the idea and tell them that Rosa was inherently kind and hospitable and she would do it for other people too.

Rosa never asked me for any assistance with benefits and entitlements. From center records, which we kept confidentially, she was receiving Social Security survivor's benefits from her deceased husband and some pension from work as waitress for many years. She had substantial income. Her apartment monthly rent was lower compared with her friends since she lived in a rent-controlled apartment.

Rosa had a habit which was disconcerting sometimes. She would collect all the cartoons of milk that the other seniors did not drink. She said she drank a lot of milk every day. She would also ask the kitchen staff for the extra food that were not served during lunch. She would always head back home with a plastic bag full of left-over food.

During monthly trips to the casinos in Atlantic City, New Jersey, a four hours ride from New York City, she would help the frail seniors get on and off the bus. Sometimes she would be offered tips from those who won in the poker games or slot machines, which she accepted with much pleasure. She hardly won any since she played only with small bets, 2 or 5 cents at the slot machines. She never played the poker and other games that required higher amount of betting. She was afraid to lose money. At least she was careful of her finances. She showed me her bank book one day when I was renewing her yearly membership at the center. It had a balance of $12,000 dollars. She was mighty proud of her adequate savings.

One day, Rosa did not come to the center, which was quite unusual. She normally would not miss any of the center activities, especially the exercise and dance classes. Perhaps she was ill, her friends said. A senior who was closest to Rosa said that she was knocking on her door at 9:00 p.m. the other night. She asked why the center was closed! Didn't she know that it was 9:00 p.m. and not 9:00 a.m.? This information got me worried. She might be suffering from Alzheimer's disease or dementia symptoms? She had not been at the center for three consecutive days.

I discussed her with my supervisor. She advised me to pay Rosa a visit at her apartment. I called first but there was no answer on her phone. That afternoon, I headed to her home. There was no response when I knocked on her door. After four failed knocking attempts, I decided to ask the apartment foreman to open her door for me. I was afraid she might be sick and could not come to the door.

I almost fainted when I entered her living area. It was in shambles. The old window curtains and drapes were tattered and yellow with age. Piles of old newspapers covered the floor of the living room area, the bedroom and the kitchen over old, gray carpet.

The few old furnishings were in disarray and were very dusty. Faded pictures with broken frames adorned the window sills, counters and side tables. There were portraits hanging on the walls precariously, as if ready to fall any minute. Rosa was nowhere in the house. The foreman left, came back and told me that the old lady went to a doctor's appointment. She had been sick.

Inside the bedroom, more horrible sights greeted me. Thicker piles of newspapers served as carpeting. The sheets smelled of urine and appeared like they had not been washed in ages. Cat litter odor merged with the urine smell. Two worn-out and dirty pillows were propped against the old, wooden headboard. There was no table lamp on the bedside table. Only a small bulb hanging over the bed was the obvious source of lighting. The two small windows were blocked with again, newspapers. I could hardly visualize someone sleeping in such miserable, deplorable sleeping quarters. I turned away from the bedroom in utter disbelief.

Now, let's go to the kitchen. Have you ever seen foodstuff tumbling out when you opened the refrigerator door? I was practically hit by cartoons of milk falling out of the old fridge when I opened it. There must had been close to two dozen cartoons of quart milk stacked inside, obviously accumulated from the center. The smell of decaying food inside the fridge was overpowering. The whole kitchen area, like the other rooms was carpeted wall to wall with old newspapers. What fire hazards!

I left the apartment, shaking my head, unable to comprehend the scenario. Rosa always looked clean, well-dressed and well made up. How could she neglect maintaining her place of abode? I asked the foreman for a duplicate key to Rosa's apartment. I dispatched a cleaning woman paid for by the agency to Rosa's house after calling and telling her of the cleaning woman's schedule for cleaning her house. The woman reported back to me that Rosa did not want her to touch her hoarded stuff.

I called one of Rosa's sons by long distance in Connecticut and asked him to visit his ailing mother. I told him to convince his mother to get rid of the fire hazards in her apartment. I followed her up with another visit the following month to tell her that I was reassigned to another center in Southwest Queens. She cried and hugged me tight for a long time.

Seniors at Woodhaven Senior Center

# Miguel

While the kids were helping their grandmother

clear up the table and the kitchen, Gabriella looked

up from the sink and said to her grandma. "I wonder

what happened to Rosa? Did you get any news about

her after you left, grandma?" "Good question, sweetie.

I learned from one of her friends that Rosa was moved

to a Nursing Home in Belmont, Queens by her sons. I

do not know what happened to her afterwards, sorry."

"Girls, would you want to hear another senior

story?" "Of course, grandma dear. It is only 8:00 p.m.

"What about the DVD that we bought from Barnes

and Noble?" Alexandra wanted to know. "All right,

girls. Let's be fair. Let's toss a coin." Grandma's story

telling prevailed. Don't worry, Alexandra. You can

watch a part of "Walker, Texas Ranger" after my story.

It is not long as the first one. They all moved to the

living room.

My next story is about Miguel, 88 years old

widower. He had been widowed for many years.

His wife of 40 years, a seamstress, died a couple

of years after he returned from Europe at the end of

World War II from a diabetic complication. He was

one of the longest participating seniors at St. Mary's

Senior Center. He claimed to have been present when

the center first opened in 1982. He was a quiet, friendly

and unassuming old man. He never participated in

any center activities, not even the card games, which

most of his friends played. All he wanted to do was

to watch the television shows, enjoy watching the

dance and exercise classes and eat congregate lunch.

After eating, he would leave immediately. He did not stay for lectures either. I learned afterwards that he only had primary education, perhaps the reason of his disinterest in educational lectures.

Miguel was very frugal. He never contributed to any center fund raising, or bought anything from our weekly flea market. He wore the same clothes almost every day. He came to the center and back home riding the bus paying only fifty cents each way. I thought that he must be very needy. I took pity on him. He always had a ready smile for me. Once or twice, he helped me unload some stuff for our flea market from my car.

One day, I saw him pay for his lunch (only (25 cents for a complete meal) with twenty five one cents.

I thought that maybe he was very needy, subsisting only on a meager Social Security income like many of our seniors. He never joined the casino trips, afraid to lose money. He would always bring home extra food for his dinner. My colleague at the center who was a volunteer saw him at the soup kitchen on Saturdays and Sundays in Woodside when our center was closed. Hearing this, I was convinced that Miguel needed help.

I asked him to see me in my office one Monday morning. I told him I was going to help him get public benefits: Food stamps, Medicaid and SSI. He had to come back to me with some proofs of income, his Security statement, pension from work if any and bank statements if any. He dutifully came back to me the following day. The proofs of income that he presented to me almost blew me away. He was getting $ 1, 175.00 dollars every month from Social Security, and $1,200.00 dollars from his company where he worked as foreman for many years. His two bank accounts showed $200,104.00 dollars balance in one bank and $55,200.00 dollars in the other. I sat there speechless for a few minutes.

Finally, I said to him. 'Miguel, you do not qualify for any benefits." I waited for his response to see what his reaction would be. May I know why not, Miss Lydia?" He seemed annoyed. I had to be very honest and frank with him. "Here are the reasons why. Your incomes from Social Security and work pension every month are well above the income eligibility limit. Your bank resources are even higher than everybody's balances, including myself. You are very rich, simply put. Your overall incomes are beyond everybody's incomes at this center combined together."

Miguel only lowered his head. After a while, he looked up and said something that surprised me.

"When is our next fundraising? I am going to donate some money. I will buy a lot of toys for your "Toys for Tots" campaign this Christmas. And Miss Lydia, next week, the 8th of the month will be my 87th birthday. I shall pay for all the seniors' lunch for two days. Is that allowed?" "Of course. Nobody is barred from doing good works here and everywhere else. Thanks so much, Miguel. You are so generous." I patted his shoulders.

Next day, Ramon and Rudy, Miguel's two closest friends came to my office with a large and heavy package. "Miguel asked us to deliver this to you." "What is it?" I was surprised at the same time curious of what was inside. "Please open it for me, Ramon." The opened box revealed a large brand new color Samsung television. I was overwhelmed with delight. Miguel probably got tired watching the news and shows from our old, small television set every day when he arrived at the center. The TV set adorned the center's community room from then on. It bore an inscription that said "Donated by Miguel, our most generous member."

## Carmen and Janet

Carmen and Janet were sisters. They lived in an apartment complex across our center. Janet, 80 years old, was a regular attendee and was one of the active center volunteers. Carmen, 83, came every once in a while. She claimed she was always busy attending to her businesses. She had five apartments for rent in Long Island City, a newspaper distribution outlet and a cafeteria in Astoria, New York.

The two were not the best of sisters. Sometimes Janet would show up at the center with swollen eyes from crying. Her close friend and neighbor, Andrea told me that the two were often at each other's throats. Janet lived in the apartment next to Carmen's on the second floor of the apartment complex. Carmen had rented the two bedroom apartment to Janet after their mother died for $600.00, a much reduced price

compared with the other apartment rents in the block.

One day, a flea market day, which Janet

managed, she did not come to the center. I sent a

messenger to her apartment with a note to Janet. The

messenger did not get a reply from her, but Janet told

him to tell me that she was ill. I sent her two meals,

one for lunch and the other for her dinner. I planned

to see her the following day. However, Janet came

just before lunch time, looking frail. She said she

was feeling better, but was coughing intermittently. I

asked her not to volunteer in the serving of lunch for

fear of contamination.

After my last client for the day, I saw Janet waiting outside my office. I beckoned to her to come in. She hardly sat down when she started her story. She and her sister had another quarrel on the same issue: the heating of her apartment. Carmen had the thermometer controlled and she would always put the temps down to 65 degrees, too cold for her sister during the fall and winter times. This was the second week of December and the temps outside were constantly down to 35 to 40 degrees Farenheit.

She complained to her sister many times about the problem, asking for the required temperature of 68 to 70 degrees room temperature. But Carmen was adamant and asked Janet to move out from her dwelling of 15 years. She said further that she was increasing her rent by $100.00 dollars more if she did not stop complaining. Janet was now crying. I stood up and came around to her and put my two hands on her shoulders. "Janet, please calm down. I might be able to help you solve your problem. Tell your sister to come to my office tomorrow after lunch time. I shall talk to both of you."

Janet refused to talk to her sister, so I sent our messenger to Carmen with a note to come and see me the following day. Carmen did not respond to my note, but two days afterwards, she came right after lunchtime. I summoned Janet who was counting the lunch money with the center treasurer, one of her daily volunteer duties. I seated them side by side in front of me. I began without so much ado.

"Ladies, I should like to hear directly from you about your troubles that I have been hearing about." Carmen started without hesitation. "My dear sister here has been giving me a lot of trouble. She puts on her television in high volume, is always behind in her rent and leaves her lights on throughout the night. She has forgotten that I have to pay the electricity, gas and air conditioner. She complains a lot, and drives me crazy. I do not want to live every day under stress. I have.....Janet interrupted. "Now, wait a minute, give me a chance to talk. I would only put on my TV high when she is not in her apartment. She knows I am on a fixed income from a small Social Security pension. I am behind in rent sometimes, but I always paid after I get my SS check. I could not sleep without the light on, you know that, my arrogant sister."

"Ha! Indeed! You make it all sound so pitiful. For what?" She stood up and glared at her younger sister, hands on her hips. Janet also stood up defiantly. "I get sick all the time because you put down the temperature very low, you mean person!" At this point, I had to intervene. "I think I have heard enough, ladies. There must be another way to resolve this problem other than through a shouting match. Kindly wait outside, Carmen. I should like to talk to your sister alone."

I closed the door after Carmen and addressed Janet in a low, sympathetic tone. "You two should not be living close to each other, don't you think, Janet? If you both continue your troubled relationship, both of you could end up with the police, in court, or you in the women's shelter, or Carmen in an insane asylum. Neither of you I'm sure would want any of that to happen." Janet broke down. I gave her a moment to calm down.

Afterwards, she looked up to me and said. "So what should I do, Miss Lydia? I have no other place to go. My apartment has been my home for a long time and I would be scared to move to some place else."

"Give me a little time, dear. Meanwhile, stay out of trouble as much as you can." When I let her out, she hugged me and thanked me.

Carmen was at the community room when I was ready for her. I called her via intercom. When she appeared at the doorway, I met her halfway to my table. "Carmen, do be seated. "How long has this problem been going on with you and your sister, Carmen? I asked gently. She was silent for a second and then she broke down, unusual for a seemingly tough woman.

"My dear husband died a few years before you came to work at the center. Since then, I had been saddled with a lot of responsibilities, which I am having a hard time coping. My children are very demanding too. My sister is only augmenting my problems instead of trying to understand me." When she posed, I said. "Carmen, understanding comes both ways. Perhaps you could spare a little consideration to your needy sister? She is not as financially lucky as you are." "I am only expecting the normal things from her. Her rent is even much lower than what the other renters are paying me. Besides the cost of everything

have all gone up. My energy bills are up and my taxes

have gone up considerably too. She should see and

understand my predicament."

"So what do you expect her to do, Carmen?"

"The only solution I would like is for her to move out

of my apartment. The sooner the better for both of

us." She declared with finality. I did not comment on

her statement but in my mind, I had already decided

the next step I would take to end up the problem once

and for all." After thanking Carmela and seeing her

off, I called the Human Resources Administration,

Section 8 Unit. I spoke with Miss Linda Johnson,

the Manager. She advised me to file an application for Janet immediately while there were still a few vacancies. I took a Section 8 Application form from my drawer and started filling out most of the sections. The rest had to be filled out by Janet.

I called in Janet the following day. She was first against the idea of moving out, but after I told her that she had no other alternatives if she wanted a peaceful life, she relented. She completed the form and signed it. I had the form delivered personally by our messenger to Miss Johnson at her office in Jamaica, Queens. Miss Johnson assigned her application a wait list number. It took three months before Janet was called for an interview. It was an expedited process pushed through by my constant follow-up and advocacy with Johnson. Some applicants had to wait for months or a year waiting period.

Carmen offered to pay for the moving van for her sister to relocate to Maplewood Section 8 Apartments on Van Wyck Expressway. That was nice of her. It was close to Richmond Hill Senior Center, our sister center in Southwest Queens. When I paid Janet a follow up visit after she had settled, she appeared happy with her new abode. She continued her volunteer work at Richmond Hill Senior Center, a walking distance from her apartment.

"Grandma, the more I listen to your senior stories, the more interested I am to be a social worker some day and work at senior centers like you." "Why, that's wonderful, sweetie. I told you before and I will tell you now girls that the job of helping people gives you great satisfaction. I would encourage you, Alexandra dear to pursue your ambition." Grandma turned to the other two girls seated opposite her on the couch. "What about, Stephanie? Gabriella?

"I would like to be a writer one day like you, grandma. Next year, I shall be graduating from high school and I intend to take up Journalism. Apart from writing, I also intend to take up Public Speaking. Maybe that would lead me to become a radio announcer or talk show host, like you too, grandma." Wow! I am very delighted, girls that you intend to follow your grandmother's legacy."How about my Gabriella?"

"Grandma, my daddy would like me to take up Medicine, which he said was his ambition when he was young. My mom would like to see me become an Architect or Engineer because she said Medicine is already common in our families." "Sweetie, although your parents' wishes are sound and good for you, take what interests you most. That is vital to success." "I am still thinking about it, grandma."

"Now, girls, it is only fifty minutes past eight o'clock. I should like to tell you another senior story which is even shorter than the previous one. This story is about a senior who was the first volunteer at the center when it opened, an 86 years old man of Irish ancestry.

# George

On the very first day of my job at St. Mary's Senior Center, one of the first senior centers in New York, George was the first man I met. He was standing at the library door on the ground floor of the four story, old building. I greeted him politely and asked him to direct me to the Site Manager's office. He looked me up and down as if assessing me. "I gave him my full name, half-expecting him to change his unwelcome attitude. "I am the center's new Case Manager."

"Wait here for a few minutes. He said rather sternly. He came back later with a tall, lean man probably in his mid-fifties. "Hi! Miss, I have been expecting you. Welcome to the center! I am Raul, Site Manager." He said enthusiastically, shaking my right hand. "Follow me to my office on the second floor. We have an elevator but I prefer to walk up and down the stairs. Good exercise, you know." He said while we were going up the staircase.

"This is my room. That is my secretary/ treasurer's room, pointing to the adjacent room. Yours is next to the secretary's room. Later, I will show you the whole center. First, let's settle down. I handed him my papers: the letter of recommendation from my supervisor at the Food And Nutrition Program where I came from, my Performance Records for the past three years and my Resume, the papers he had asked me to bring. He read my credentials one by one.

"You have very good performance ratings. And oh, you have a high educational qualification. I am very impressed. You will be an asset to the center. I am very happy to have someone like you to work with us." He stood up and led me to my assigned office.

"Be comfortable working here, Lydia. May I call you by your first name? "Of course. I would much prefer it sir." He toured me around the place after he had introduced the chef and the workers in the kitchen. He showed me the community room, the library, the dining area and the balcony in the back.

We went back to the second floor. This is the supervisor's room. He pointed to a bigger, well-furnished room opposite my room. "She comes only once a week. She is expected back tomorrow. The adjacent one to hers is for the interns. Our secretary, Shirley is off today. The room at the corner is the volunteers' room. The third floor is vacant right now. We are using two rooms there for storage. The top floor is open for renting. Meanwhile, it is used occasionally to house seniors who do not have air conditioners at home during the height of the summer and have no heat during the very cold winter days."

Back downstairs, he introduced me to Leo and George, sitting behind a booth. Leo, a paid staff, handled the lunch money. George was in charge of handing out the lunch tickets after they had been paid. The price of lunch tickets was $25 cents. The senior lunches, which were well-balanced were mostly subsidized by the Dept. for the Aging. George did not even look at me. He was as rude as when I first met him. Leo on the other hand was very polite and welcoming.

Every day I reported to work, George would be by the library door, watching me but would not say anything. I had the feeling that he did not like me at all. I became curious about this man who had no nice words to say to me. I took out the center records and looked him up. He was a widower of twelve years, had only one son who was married without children living in Boston area. He lived in a rent-controlled apartment near Queensboro Bridge in Queens. He had a low income from Social Security and would qualify for public benefits. I was happy knowing that he might need my help after all. We could be friends.

I went to the library one day not to read or borrow a book but to have a chance to speak to him. He was coughing and looked sick. George, are you feeling o.k.?" He did not say anything to me but when I turned to leave, he spoke with a hoarse voice. "Thanks for asking, Miss Lydia. I only have a little cold. I saw an opportunity to speak to him about my intention. I sat opposite him at the table and said earnestly.

"I would like to help you, George." "I don't think I need any help, Miss." "Do you know that there are many benefits and entitlements available to you if you are interested, George?' "Like what?

He demanded. "Like Food Stamps, Medicaid, SSI

and other benefits too. That's my job here, to help

seniors get what they qualify for." He stood up from

his chair slowly and looking at me straight in the eye,

he said. "I am not a beggar, Miss. I do not want you to

help me with anything, especially dole outs from the

government. Just leave me be." With those words, he

strode outside slowly. I did not see him again that day.

After that conversation, George seemed more

amiable. He would say Hi! when we bumped into

each other in hallways. I was content with that, but I

resented his refusal to apply for benefits. He seemed

a very proud man. I owed him respect, especially that he appeared more sickly and frail. I spoke to the site manager about him. He said what I already concluded. He was a very proud man, but was a very helpful center volunteer. We both agreed to leave him be.

I did not see George for a few days. He was a fixture at the center, so when he did not come for four consecutive days, everyone was concerned. We sent a messenger to check on him. When he came back, he went straight to the site manager. I could hear him talking excitedly to Mr. Raul. Mr. Raul came to me looking very sad.

"Lydia, I have bad news. The messenger told me that he found George slumped near his bed, dead, obviously for a couple of days now. His apartment had an awful smell, Marcos said. He is still in shock. Please contact his son immediately in Boston." I said a prayer and went about my task feeling very sorry for George. His body was brought to the morgue. The site manager declared a state of mourning at the center for the long time, hard-working volunteer. The son, Andrew came and buried him in Boston.

"That was a sad story, grandma. Did many of your seniors die while you were working with them?" Stephanie asked. "Yes. We had deaths every year, some brought to Nursing Homes and others just ceased coming for reasons we never knew. Visiting hospitals, nursing homes, attending wakes and attending funerals were so much part of my duties.""

"Do you still want to become a social worker, Alexandra?" Gabriella nudged her cousin who had her hands on her cheeks. "I will have to think about it real hard," she replied uncertainly. "Well, you still have two years to think about it, right, sis?" Grandma went closer to her granddaughters and said lovingly. "Girls nothing or no one should force you to pursue a career you don't like, remember that. Let's head to bed now. It's almost ten o'clock!"

"What are we going to do tomorrow, granny?"

Gabriella wanted to know. "In the morning, we shall

do food shopping after breakfast. I would like to show

Stephanie how to make Pot Roast and Leche Plan

dessert." We can go to Randall Rd. in the afternoon

to the shopping malls to shop for items you want

grandma to buy for you and for your moms. "Sounds

very good, grandma. Goodnight, dearest granny."

They kissed their grandma one by one.

# Cindy

The following night, while grandma and her three grandchildren were about to sit down to dinner, grandma called the girls' attention:

"Girls, I would like to tell two more short senior stories now, while we are eating dinner. Tomorrow, your aunt and uncle are going to pick you up. This is our last story telling night until next time you are here, hopefully next year. The first one is about Cindy, an 81 year-old widow.

Cindy was a persistent, demanding client who came to see me almost every day. She would complain about the day's lunch, the bad weather, about her neighbor's dog, the mail man whom she said stole her Social Security check and about anything, everything else. One day, I told her that I had other clients who needed urgent help. "Cindy, come here once a week from now on, and only when you need help." I think she resented that. She did not come to my office for two weeks in a row. After lunch which she did not miss every day, I would see her sitting on the porch or in the family room watching television with the other seniors.

She did not participate in my exercise and dance classes either. I surmised that she was a very sensitive and insecure old lady. Somehow, I was relieved that she did not bother me anymore. One afternoon, she barged into my room, sat down without being told and cried. 'What's the matter, Cindy?" I went around and held both her hands. She continued to cry even louder. "It's my daughter, Merriam. She threw me out of her house. She got so angry when I discovered that all my bank savings were wiped out. She said that she had nothing to do with it. Who else would have done it? She is my only co-depositor." She continued to weep.

"Look, Cindy. Has she been talking money from your account before this? "Yes. Not only that. Every time I would complain about withdrawals that

I did not do, she would hit me and tell me I was a useless being, that all I do is complain and that she wished I would die." Oh, that's terrible! "Calm down." I gave her a glass of water. I immediately thought of something. Cindy has to move out of that abusive environment. I suggested that she stay with a friend, Rose who lived alone and had a spare bedroom. I took her to Rose' house and requested her to allow Cindy to remain with her until I arranged something.

I called the Elder Abuse Hotline and reported the abuse. We worked together in relocating Cindy to a women's shelter in Flushing while an Elder Law lawyer proceeded to take action against the abusive daughter. After a lot of advocacy and referrals, the daughter went to court and was recommended a prison term. The woman posted bail and moved to her aunt's house in Forest Hills.

Cindy did not like the Women's Shelter. She said that the situation there was crowded and that their meals and accommodation were awful. Knowing Cindy as an ever complaining person, I decided to have her move to an Assisted Living Facility in Woodhaven. The application process was long and difficult. Good that Cindy had no more bank account to disqualify her to settle in a city-funded facility. I worked tirelessly to get her Medicaid benefits.

The Woodhaven Assisted Living Program accepted only those who had Medicaid. Her survivor's benefit from Social Security was a bit over the income limit. Her $450.00 income from her former job as a cleaner in a school added up also. I convinced Cindy to get whatever amount was left from her pension in lump sum and put it into the facility as a down payment. Again, I did a lot of maneuvers to get around the system. Finally, after almost a year, Cindy was accepted and was given a room that she shared with another old lady. I visited her occasionally and I saw that she appeared happy.

I got a shock one morning when I got a call from the manager of Woodhaven Assisted Living Facility. Cindy died in her sleep last night. She appeared to be asleep, according to her room mate. When she failed to show up for breakfast and did not attend the Bingo game, which she usually did not miss, her roommate tried to wake her up. That was when they knew she was dead. She had a heart attack in her sleep. I felt miserable. My only consolation was that I did what I could for the poor, old woman."

"Another sad story, right, girls?" The girls continued to eat in silence. "Perhaps it would cheer you up to hear my next story. In the meantime, let's

finish up and move into the living room.

Author with seniors at St. Mary Senior Center

# Ricardo

Ricardo was born in Uruguay but was brought by her American father and Hispanic mother to America when he was little. He never went to visit his country of origin for some reason. His records showed that he was a sergeant in the Army and served during the last year of World War II in England. He got married to a teacher and had two children, a boy and a girl. His wife died in a train accident during a trip to the Grand Canyon in Arizona ten years back. His children both got families of their own. One lived in Ohio, the other in Texas. Ricardo was a jolly, active 85 year old senior. He never missed to participate in all the center activities. He liked to dance and to sing. I asked him to lead a singing activity when I had to excuse myself to attend to a client who had an emergency. My client, Lourdes' daughter was injured in a motorbike accident on Van Wyck Expressway driven by her boyfriend. The boyfriend died at the scene, but Rita survived the crash with serious injuries. Her chances of recovery from unconsciousness was uncertain. Lourdes needed someone's shoulder to cry on, which I provided, along with words of comfort. I took her to Queens Hospital where her daughter was, on my way home that day.

Ricardo did a good job leading the seniors singing old songs from the 40's. I could hear his voice above the others from my office upstairs above the community room. He was a good leader. He had a good sense of humor too. He was generally liked especially by the ladies. I urged him to be a volunteer in conducting the singing and the dancing classes. He could dance almost all the classic dances, the Tango, Cha Cha, Rumba and Twist. He gladly accepted the offer. I was now relieved of some of my activities and able to concentrate on my office duties.

In the fall of 2002, my elder sister came to visit me and Joe. She came from her son and family's home in Toronto, Canada. After half a year stay in Canada, she came to the U.S. before going back home to

Manila. She remained with us for two months instead of five months because her husband was seriously ill. He died of a lingering illness soon after her return.

My sister Precy was a very good dancer. She was the darling in our family of six children, very pretty, intelligent and friendly. She had a degree in Journalism and was a contributor to a newspaper company in Metro Manila. She would go with me to work every day since she did not want to be alone in the house. Joe was still working then and we saw each other only in the evening during dinner times.

Ricardo showed a liking for my sister soon after I introduced her to him. I think my sister also liked him. They partnered during the dance activity twice

a week. My sister was never a singer so she would

only watch and listen to the group singing led by

Ricardo. During the monthly birthday party for the

celebrants of the month, the two were inseparable

dance partners. They also ate together during lunch.

Everybody was curious and watched the two together

everyday.

Ricardo approached me one morning when I

arrived. Without my sister's hearing, he asked me. "Is

your sister married?' I briefly said "Yes." He was a bit

sad but he did not change his special attention to my

sister. My sister and I discussed him when we were

heading home one afternoon. "Ricardo is a terribly nice man." I said, concentrating on the busy traffic on Queens Blvd. "Indeed he is. He reminds me of my husband, Jake. He was a terrific dancer too once upon a time." We were silent for a while. Half the way home after navigating through heavy traffic on the Expressway, she suddenly said. "You know, Ricardo proposed. I told him I was married but he insisted that I could get a divorce if I liked him enough."

I was not surprised. He had hinted it and I had half expected he would propose one day. One weekend, on my sister's second month, an overnight letter arrived. It came from Ricardo addressed to my Manang Precy care of me. When she opened it, two $100.00 dollar bills came tumbling from inside the envelope. A note that accompanied the bills said briefly: "This is for you both, a Christmas gift from me," signed Ricardo.

I looked at my sister and told her. "We have to return this money. We are not allowed to receive money from our clients. Would you like to keep yours?" "Oh no. I am not used to receiving money from a man, any man for that matter." She handed the two bills to me. "I am going to return this tomorrow by the same way it came." I wrote a small note thanking the generous giver and telling him honestly why we were returning

it. I posted it the following day.

When my sister had to leave urgently to attend

to her ailing husband, Ricardo did not come to the

center for many days. When he showed up for lunch

a week afterwards, he appeared intoxicated. I called

him into my office. "Ricardo, I would like to remind

you in my capacity as the case manager of this center

that the senior members can attend the center only

when they are sober. We have a memo on the subject.

I should like you to read it before you leave." I handed

a handbook to him. He declined to read the memo.

"I am sorry, Miss Lydia. It won't happen again."

He apologized and left. He seldom ever came to the center afterwards until he ceased to come entirely.

"That was still another sad story, grandma. He must have cared so much for our grand aunt that he did not want to come to your center any longer and be reminded of her." "That was a really nice comment, Stephanie. I feel like hearing it from a well-grown up lady." "Grandma, did our grand aunt Precy come back to visit you again in New York?"

"No dear. She developed cancer of the uterus and died two years after her first and last visit. It was on stage 3." "Now, that was another sad story, even more sad than any of the ones you have told us, right? Stephanie? Alexandra?" Gabriella declared. The two girls nodded sadly.

Grandma was about to leave her grandchildren's bedroom after kissing them goodnight when Stephanie sat up and said, "I forgot to mention to you, grandma dear that I am graduating from high school six months from now, in March next year. My mom is going to invite you, my daddy and his wife and uncle Glynn and his family. Are you coming, grandma?"

"Of course, darling. I would never miss that important event for anything. My first granddaughter's graduation! I can hardly believe how fast time went. I will also stay with Olivia and Brian in Tampa for four

or five days." "Very good, grandma. Then you can

tell us more senior stories. Hearing about the seniors'

problems and how you assisted and empathized with

them will help me decide if I am going to take up

Social Work after graduation from high school."

"Wonderful! But sweetie, when do you expect

to finish high school?" In two years time, hopefully."

Then your cousin Gabriella will be graduating on

the same year as well, right?" Gabriella who seemed

asleep turned and said sleepily. "Yes, my sweet

grandma. I hope to graduate on the same year as my

dear cousin here, Alexandra. That is if she does not

get married before then." Alexandra gave Gabriella

Alexandra, Gabriella, and Stephanie

a little push and declared. "Never! I pledge not to

get married until I graduate and have a job. I do not

even have a boyfriend yet."" "Alexandra, don't make

pledges you are not sure to keep," a rebuke from her

older sister."

"And grandma, I would like you to stay with

us at our home for a couple of days at least when you

go to Miami to attend Stephanie's graduation. My

mom and Dad would be delighted to have you. Then

perhaps you can tell some of your senior stories to

them too." "Yes, darling. I intend to. I have not been

to your house since last year. Is your ferret still there?

"Sadly, no. He died after my dad bathed him. We

suspected he died of pneumonia." "A pity! When I

was there, I saw that your dad was very fond of him!

"Indeed he was. He could not get over with it for some time. We plan to get a dog one day."

"Now, girls, you go to sleep now. My going to Miami in March is now firmly settled." "We are anxious to hear more of your senior stories, remember, dearest granny." Alexandra emphasized. The girls took turns in kissing their grandmother goodnight again.

The following afternoon, Bing and Ariel came to pick up the girls. Grandma went with them to her daughter's and son in-law's house. She spent dinner with them and watched a movie with the kids, "Friendly Persuasion," a film good for the whole family.

Grandma Lydia went to the airport with Bing and her grandchildren to see the girls off a week afterwards. It had been a happy week for everyone but grandma Lydia was lonely again after they had left, as she always was after spending time with her precious grandchildren.

Two weeks before Stephanie's graduation day, she received a phone call from Clyde, her son, the father of Stephanie and Alexandra. It was already half past ten in the evening, time for bed. "Mom! Hope you are still awake!" He sounded very excited. "I called earlier but your line was always busy. You would be happy to hear my news. Stephanie is one of the Cum Laude students among the more than a thousand graduating students at Miami Dade High School. I received a congratulatory note this afternoon from her principal and an invitation to a party for the school's "high achievers" after the graduation ceremonies."

"Goodness me! That's terrific news! Congratulations, my dear son! Stephanie obviously has inherited your exceptional educational achievements. I have to send her a congratulatory card by special delivery." "No Mom, this is supposed to be a surprise for you and for the others, but I could not contain myself. When you get to Miami for her graduation, just act as if you did not know anything, all right, mom?"

"O.K. dear. As you wish. Oh, I am so overjoyed I can't possibly sleep tonight." "Goodnight, mom and try to sleep well. We shall see you at the graduation ceremony in two weeks. Vika is saying hello to you." "Say the same to her son. How is her new job? "Terrific. Goodnight now."

Lydia Bongcaron Wade, Author

With her Grandchildren Olivia and Brian (top);

Gabriella, Stephanie, and Alexandra (below)

"Where Miracles Grow," June 13, 2012

"Grandma Series I, October 22, 2012

"Grandma Series II, April 19, 2013

"Love Born on the High Seas," June 9, 2014

"Love Born in the War Front," Jan. 28, 2015

"Literary Gems," June 23, 2016

"Grandma Series III," July 15, 2016